Fun Facts for the EFL/ESL Classroom
A Teacher's Resource Book

Stephen Mark Silvers

Retired, Federal University of Amazonas
Manaus, Amazonas, Brazil

Fun Facts for the EFL/ESL Classroom: A Teacher's Resource Book.

Copyright © by Stephen Mark Silvers, 2021

All rights reserved. No part of this book may be used or reproduced in any manner whatsoever for commercial purposes. However, permission is hereby granted for teachers to reproduce parts for use in their classrooms.

Cover by author and Top Notch Copy & Print

ISBN: 978-0-578-86750-2

Contents

A. Introduction **1**

B. Part One: Facts presented in sets **8**
    1. Set A **9**
    2. Set B **19**
    3. Set C **29**
    4. Set D **39**
    5. Set E **49**
    6. Set F **59**

C. Part Two: Facts presented by topics. **69**

D. Appendices **135**
    1. Animals **136**
    2. Countries **137**
    3. People **139**
    4. Vocabulary for *The Global Table* **143**
    5. Vocabulary for *Breakfast around the World* **144**

E. Resources **145**

F. Acknowledgments **149**

G. About the author **150**

Contents for Part Two

1. Animal champions **70**
2. Animal curiosities **73**
3. The global table **76**
4. Breakfast around the world **78**
5. Exotic foods **80**
6. Weather extremes **81**
7. Natural wonders **82**
8. Man-made landmarks **84**
9. Environmental concerns **86**
10. Sporting countries **88**
11. Fun country facts **89**
12. City curiosities **93**
13. Cultural do's and don'ts **95**
14. New Year's traditions **97**
15. Birthdays around the world **99**
16. Young achievers **103**
17. Older achievers **105**
18. Interesting people **107**
19. Curious deaths **113**
20. Death by stupidity **115**
21. Funny tombstones **117**
22. Bizarre laws **118**
23. Strange lawsuits **120**
24. Stupid thieves **122**
25. Unusual books **124**
26. Crazy song titles **125**
27. Superstitions **126**
28. Curious inventions **128**
29. When was it invented? **129**
30. Unsolved mysteries **131**

Introduction

Fun Facts is a teacher's resource book of over 1,000 facts that can be used to:

- ➢ provide a quick filler
- ➢ set a relaxed atmosphere conducive to learning
- ➢ bring a little fun and humor to a lesson
- ➢ add variety and provide a change of pace

You will find facts that are educational, entertaining, amusing, funny, curious, strange, hard-to-believe, and even bizarre. There are facts about the environment, animals, nature, space and the universe, countries, cities, culture and customs from around the world, famous and lesser-known people, and much more.

Fun Facts can be used with teens, young adults, and adults, beginning with the second book of a basic four-book series. This means that students would be at (at least) a low A-2 level of the CEFR (Common European Framework of Reference) and would have had around 100 (or more) hours of previous English language classroom instruction.

Organization and contents

The book is divided into two parts. In Part One, the facts are arranged into six sets, sets A-F. All six sets are at the same level of difficulty; there isn't any increase in difficulty from one set to the next. The facts are presented in a tabular format, with each row of the table being labelled (A-1, B-1, etc.) and containing one to three related facts. Thus, the three facts presented in A-17 below are all related to the danger of smoking.

A-17	Cigarette smoke contains more than 7,000 chemicals, 70 of which are known to cause cancer. A person who smokes a pack of cigarettes a day is doing the equivalent of drinking half a cup of tar a year.

INTRODUCTION

While all the information within a row is conceptually related, there is no relationship between adjacent rows. Thus, the facts presented in rows A-16 and A-18 are completely unrelated to row A-17.

In Part Two, the facts are also presented in a tabular form, but there the facts are arranged into topics. All of the rows within a given topic present facts that are related to that topic. In addition to the topics already mentioned above, the topics in Part Two include, among others, exotic foods, younger and older achievers, stupid thieves, superstitions, and unsolved mysteries. In all, there are 30 different topics in Part Two, each one with 8 to 34 rows of related facts.

There are also five appendices and a section labelled "Resources." Appendix 1 lists all of the animals in the book, and Appendix 2 lists the countries. Each of these animals and countries has an article in the online encyclopedia Simple English Wikipedia (a good source for additional information; the articles are short and use easy-to-understand language suitable for EFL/ESL students). Appendix 3 is a list of the 258 most important people in the book. Each of them has an article in Wikipedia, and the ones marked with an asterisk* also have an article in Simple English Wikipedia. Appendices 4 and 5 list the major food vocabulary found in the topics "the global table" and "breakfast around the world."

The section labelled "Resources" provides a list of books and Internet sites that I found useful for finding interesting facts. Most of the books can be found on Amazon or on similar sites (I highly recommend Thriftbooks.com). The Internet sources have been listed in categories, such as encyclopedias and facts for kids, general fun facts, animals, people, etc. Of course, you can also make an Internet search for facts using your preferred search program typing in a phrase such as "fun facts for kids about (animals, the planet Mars, Albert Einstein, funeral customs around the world, etc.). I suggest using "kids" in the search as it will bring up facts in simpler language and with less technical and non-essential information.

INTRODUCTION

The Internet resources includes two sets of sites that are not related to facts. In "Dictionaries" you will find three online dictionaries. They can help you to understand and explain any words that you or your students are unfamiliar with. "Pronunciation help" provides the web addresses for two sites where you can type in a word (especially the name of a person, country, or a city) and hear how it is pronounced.

Style notes and related issues

With few exceptions, the contracted forms (he's, she's, it's, that's, they're, isn't, aren't) have been used throughout the book. The facts are meant to be presented to the class in an informal, conversational style, and one of the characteristics of spoken English is the prevalence of contracted forms.

The plural form "they" has been used to refer to a singular noun when it will avoid the cumbersome use of the expression "he or she." This seems to be an increasingly more common stylistic feature.

A major concern was with readability. The teacher should be able to pick up the book, take it to their class, and easily read the facts to the class. Two devices have been used to facilitate this. When a row has several sentences, they are often separated by a small black square (▪). This square is also used to signal a change of subject, as for example when there are facts about two different people, animals, countries, etc. The second device is the use of space. Extra space has been added between sentences and occasionally after commas.

Nationality and dates of birth and death have often been provided in parentheses next to a person's name. This information would not be presented in the reading of the facts; it could of course be provided later.

Units of measurement are first given in the metric system, followed in parentheses by the US standard system: kilometers (miles); meters (feet); centimeters (inches); kilos (pounds); liters (gallons). To facilitate your reading and pronunciation, these units of measurement have not been abbreviated (for example, km, cm). Of course, you will only use the system used in your country.

INTRODUCTION

Teaching options

Below you will find various options for using *Fun Facts* in your classroom. As you experiment with the materials, you will discover which options fit best with your objectives, the amount of time you wish to spend on an activity, and your own personal teaching preferences. You can:

1. use the facts as just a brief listening activity or expand the activity using some of the options presented below.

2. choose a row of facts and read all of the information with only a slight pause between sentences.

3. stop after each sentence and ask the class if it's ready for the next fact.

4. pre-teach vocabulary that you believe your students are unfamiliar with. 47

5. present the facts without pre-teaching vocabulary and then ask the class if there were any words that they didn't understand.

6. put the name of the person you're going to talk about on the board. You might then say something like, "I'm going to tell you some facts about (name of the person on the board)." This also applies to the names of countries, national dishes, etc., anything the students would not be familiar with.

7. ask the class what they know about the person, animal, thing, place, or topic you are going to talk about: "What do you know about (the Eiffel Tower)?"

8. ask the class a question whose answer is in the facts you are going to read. For example, "What's the greatest recorded human age?" The students make guesses, which can be put on the board. This works best for numerical facts, but it can also be used for other facts: "What country is known as 'the land of smiles'?" The act of guessing leads to greater student engagement.

INTRODUCTION

9. make a statement and ask the class to guess whether it is true or false. For example, "The heart of a blue whale weighs as much as a truck."

10. follow up a fact or a set of facts with a question. After you have given the fact that the average person forgets 90% of their dreams, you can ask the class if they remember their dreams. This can lead to option number 11.

11. use the facts that you presented as a springboard for conversation or debate.

12. project a picture related to the facts. The picture could be used to show what you just talked about: "Here is a picture of Beethoven." Or it could be used as a conversation starter: "What do you think of Beethoven's music? What kind of music do you listen to?" It will be easy to find pictures on the internet (Google images, Bing images).

13. show a YouTube video related to the facts. As with the suggestion for using pictures, a YouTube video can be used just to show or to serve as a conversation starter.

14. use a set of facts to practice listening comprehension.

15. devise a lesson around one of the topics in Part Two.

16. photocopy pages from the book, cut out the sets of facts, give one set to each student, and have the students present their facts to the class.

17. ask the students to find more facts about what was just presented and present them to the class.

18. Ask the students to compare two facts and say which fact they found more interesting (amusing, surprising, unbelievable).

19. Have the students prepare and perform a skit based on the facts just presented.

INTRODUCTION

Keeping track

You will want to devise a system to keep track of which sets of facts you have used with each group of students. As much as possible, you want to avoid the students hearing facts that they have already heard in a previous class. I will give an example of how this could be done in a language school that uses a four-book series, but the idea can be adapted to other situations. Here is how you could divide up the facts in Part One. (Remember, all six sets are at the same linguistic level.)

book one	not used
book two	sets A and B
book three	sets C and D
book four	sets E and F

Since each row of facts is alphanumerically identified, you can use a notebook to record which facts you have used. Another option is to record the identifying numbers in your lesson plans.

For Part Two, you could divide the 30 topics into three sets of 10, either using the order presented on page 69, or making your own selection as to which 10 topics go with each level.

book two	Topics 1-10
book three	Topics 11-20
book four	Topics 21-30

INTRODUCTION

Accuracy of the facts

I have tried to make sure the facts are accurate, often consulting more than one source. However, in many cases, even the experts don't agree. For example, different sources give different typical weights for an elephant. In those cases, I always chose what seemed to be a consensus. Cultural facts are subjective and open to questioning as to how accurate they are. Is it really true that in Kuwait when the host stands up that signals the meal is over? Also, facts change, particularly with regard to records. A man from Australia set a record of 2,806 push-ups. Maybe by the time you read this, someone will have done 3,000. *Fun Facts* is not a scientific work, and thus all the facts presented should be considered as "basically true."

Origins of the book

Almost 30 years, ago I saw an activity called "Amazing Facts" in *Five-Minute Activities: A Resource Book of Short Activities* by Penny Ur and Andrew Wright (Cambridge University Press, 1992). Years later, in 2018, at a bookstore in Seattle, I came across *The Blackbirch Kids Almanac of Geography*, which I immediately recognized as a goldmine of interesting facts for the EFL/ESL classroom. This triggered my memory of the "Amazing Facts" activity, and thus was born my interest in writing a book of fun facts.

A final word

I hope that you will have as much fun using the facts in your classroom as I had in researching and finding them. I also hope that you will find the suggested ways (options) for using the book useful and that they will stimulate your own creativity in the teaching of English as a foreign or second language.

As a final suggestion, you can take the book to a local printing establishment and have them cut the spine and rebind the book with a spiral coil. I often did this with course books when I was teaching English in Brazil and always found that it made them much easier to use in class. I highly recommend this.

Part One
Facts Presented in Sets

Set A

A-1	For every human in the world there are one million ants. ▪ There are no ants in Iceland, Greenland, or Antarctica. ▪ An ant can lift an object that is 50 times its weight. If a man were that strong, he would be able to lift three cars.
A-2	An asteroid about the size of a car enters the atmosphere roughly once a year—but it burns up before it reaches us. ▪ Once every few million years, an asteroid large enough to threaten the existence of life on Earth arrives.
A-3	The earliest stone tools were found in Ethiopia and go back an incredible 2.5 million years. ▪ The earliest use of fire by humans has been traced back approximately 1.5 million years to locations in East Africa.
A-4	Every inch (2.45 centimeters) of your skin is home to about 32 million bacteria, but the majority are harmless or even helpful. The total weight of the bacteria in the human body is about 2 kilos (4 pounds).
A-5	Jeanne Calment (1875–1997) had the longest human lifespan. She lived to the age of 122 years, 164 days. ▪ She loved her cigarettes and only quit smoking at the age of 117. ▪ On her 120th birthday, she was asked what kind of future she expected. Her reply was: "A very short one."
A-6	When some men tried to abduct a 12-year-old Ethiopian girl to force her into marriage, a group of three lions chased off her attackers, waited with her until the police came, and then retreated back into the forest.

SET A

A-7	Bobby Leach (1858–1926) survived going over Niagara Falls in a wooden barrel but died several months later after slipping on a banana peel. ▪ French playwright Molière became ill and died while playing the role of the hypochondriac in his play *The Imaginary Invalid*.
A-8	The Amazon River is 6,400 kilometers (4,000 miles) long (slightly shorter than the Nile). ▪ At its mouth, it's nearly as wide as the Thames River is long. ▪ It empties 219 million liters (58 million gallons) of water into the Atlantic Ocean every second.
A-9	In 1998, England lost to Argentina in a World Cup penalty shootout. On that day, and for two days afterwards, the number of heart attacks in England increased by 25%. ▪ In 1964, a soccer match between Peru and Argentina ended in a riot in which 318 people died.
A-10	Herbert Fisher and Zelmyra Fisher were married in May of 1924. They had been married 86 years, 290 days when Mr. Fisher passed away. ▪ One of the shortest marriages was that of pop singer Britney Spears to her childhood friend Jason Alexander. It lasted a mere 55 hours.
A-11	There's a cemetery in Japan that features a lifelike robotic replica of a Buddhist priest with blinking eyes that chants over the dead each morning. ▪ In 1991, a company in Sydney, Australia, began making "ecologically safe" coffins out of recycled newspapers.
A-12	How many grilled-cheese sandwiches do you think you could eat in one minute? The record is 13. ▪ How many peanut butter and jelly sandwiches do you think you could eat in one minute? The record is 6.

SET A

A-13	The hot dog originated in Germany as a dachshund sausage. ▪ In the 19th century in North America, it was placed in a long bread roll and called a "hot dog." ▪ The name "hot dog" came from vendors who were selling the sausage, calling out, "Get your dachshund sausages while they're red hot."
A-14	Aloha Wanderwell (1906–1996) was the first person to drive around the world. ▪ She traveled across 80 countries in a Ford Model T, starting and ending in Nice, France. ▪ The journey began when she was just 16 years old and took five years to complete (1922–1927).
A-15	In 2014, Dutch cyclist Maarten de Jonge changed his flight to an earlier option. He was lucky because his original flight crashed. And he was lucky a second time. Later that same year, he again changed flights, and again the original flight crashed.
A-16	In the year 2020, the five most populated cities (in round numbers) were: **1.** Tokyo (37,000,000) **2.** New Delhi (29,000,000) **3.** Shanghai (26,000,000) **4.** São Paulo (21,850,000) **5.** Mexico City (21,700,000)
A-17	Cigarette smoke contains more than 7,000 chemicals, 70 of which are known to cause cancer. A person who smokes a pack of cigarettes a day is doing the equivalent of drinking half a cup of tar a year.
A-18	The tallest residential–only building is 432 Park Avenue in New York City. It's 85 stories high and has 104 condominium units. Apartments begin at $7 million. ▪ The tallest hotel in the world is the 75-story Gevora Hotel in Dubai.

SET A

A-19	In 2011, French daredevil climber Alain Robert, known as "the French Spiderman," scaled the Burj Khalifa Tower in Dubai with nothing more than climbing shoes, chalk for his hands, and a safety harness. It took him six hours to scale the 162-story tower.
A-20	The *Victoria Regia*, a giant water lily found in the Amazon, has 2.5 meter (8 foot) wide leaves that can easily support the weight of a small child. ▪ The giant Redwood trees of California reach a height of 113 meters (371 feet). That's as tall as a 37-story building.
A-21	Winston Churchill (1874–1965) used to pet black cats to obtain good luck. ▪ Napoleon (1769–1821) was afraid of cats and the number 13. ▪ Author Charles Dickens (1812–1870) always faced north when he slept. ▪ US president Harry Truman (1884–1972) had a horseshoe over the door of his office at the White House.
A-22	Some people have odd jobs: a Bonecrusher attends the machine that crushes animal bones used in the manufacture of glue. ▪ An Egg Smeller smells eggs after they are broken open to check for spoilage. ▪ A Queen Producer raises queen bees.
A-23	Hummingbirds visit as many as 1,000 flowers each day. ▪ The bee hummingbird of Cuba is the world's smallest bird. They're so small that they are often mistaken for insects. They hover by flapping their wings 80 times a second.
A-24	The heaviest human ever was Jon Minnoch (1941–83). He weighed more than 640 kilos (1,400 pounds). That's about the same as a Holstein cow. He was buried in a double-size wooden coffin that took up two spaces in the cemetery.

SET A

A-25	Pluto was discovered in 1930 by Clyde Tombaugh (1906 –1997), an American astronomer. ▪ It was named after the Greek god of the underworld. ▪ The name was suggested by an 11-year-old girl from England.
A-26	Octavio Guillen and Adriana Martinez of Mexico were engaged for 67 years. They were both 15 years old when they became engaged and 82 years old on their wedding day. ▪ Beverly Redmond (UK) finally agreed to marry her husband, Keith, after he had made 8,500 proposals in 24 years.
A-27	On the average, Americans consume 26 liters (7 gallons) of ice cream every year; Australians consume 18 liters (5 gallons); and Danes, 9 liters (2 gallons). ▪ On the average, Americans eat 300 cookies every year, or about 35,000 over a lifetime.
A-28	In 2005, Englishman Tim FitzHigham rowed across the English Channel in a bathtub in just over 9 hours. ▪ In 2019, Frenchman Franky Zapata crossed the English Channel in 22 minutes riding on his jet-propelled Flyboard/hoverboard.
A-29	The bride at a gypsy wedding in Italy traditionally smashes a pottery jar over the groom's head. ▪ In Venezuela, it's considered good luck if the newlyweds can sneak out of the reception party without being seen. ▪ In Bali, the groom helps his bride cook the entire wedding feast.
A-30	Coca-Cola was first marketed in 1886 as a nerve tonic that relieves exhaustion. ▪ It sold 25 bottles its first year. Today, it sells 1.8 billion bottles—per day. ▪ On the average, over 10,000 soft drinks from Coca-Cola are consumed every second of every day globally.

SET A

A-31	The adult human heart is about the size of a fist. ▪ It beats about 72 times a minute. 100,000 times a day. 42 million times a year. ▪ Every day it pumps the equivalent of 38,000 glasses of water through your body. This is like lifting a weight of 10 tons to a height of 10 meters (33 feet) every day.
A-32	One couple from Belgium got married on top of a bungee-jumping platform 48 meters (160 feet) high. That's as high as a 16-story building. ▪ A couple from New York were married underwater dressed in wetsuits inside a protective cage in a shark tank, surrounded by sharks.
A-33	The Uape Indians of the Upper Amazon mix the ashes of their dead with a local fermented beverage. The resulting drink is passed around to be enjoyed, along with tales of the departed's life and accomplishments.
A-34	In 2014, Alan Eustace (USA), a senior vice president at Google, parachuted from a helium-filled balloon at an altitude of 41,400 meters (136,000 feet). That's three times higher than the normal altitude of a jet passenger plane.
A-35	In Taiwan, garbage trucks play classical music by Beethoven to signal their arrival. ▪ In Uganda, in setting a time for meeting someone, you need to clarify if you are using normal time or Uganda time, which can be one or two hours after the set time.
A-36	What do Leonardo da Vinci, Alexander the Great, and the Boston Strangler have in common? They were all left-handed. ▪ What do Charles Darwin and Abraham Lincoln have in common? They were both born on February 12, 1809.

SET A

A-37	Santa Claus, also known Saint Nicholas, is based on a real Saint Nicholas who was born in what is now present-day Turkey ▪ In 1996, the first successfully cloned mammal, a sheep named Dolly, was created in Scotland at the University of Edinburgh.
A-38	The record for being covered by bees is held by Ruan Liangming (China). His entire body was covered by 637,000 bees, weighing 63 kilos (140 pounds). ▪ Johannes Relleke, a tin miner in Rhodesia (now Zimbabwe), was stung 2,443 times and survived.
A-39	The tallest man ever was Robert Wadlow (1918 –1940). He was 2.72 meters (8 feet 11 inches) tall. ▪ At his shoulder, he was taller than the front door of his house. ▪ His shoes were 47 centimeters (18 inches) long. ▪ At the age of 5, he was taller than his mother. ▪ At the age of 9, he was strong enough to carry his father on his back up the stairs to the second floor.
A-40	A British couple, Bertie and Jessie Wood, divorced and ended their 36-year marriage when they were both 98 years old and just a few years away from their 100th birthdays. The reason for the split is not known.
A-41	How many push-ups can you do? Jarrad Young of Australia did 2,806 nonstop push-ups in one hour. That's 46 push-ups every minute. ▪ Jarrad is also the record holder for push-ups with claps. He did 1,164 push-ups, clapping once between each push-up.
A-42	After George D. Bryson checked in at his hotel in Kentucky, the clerk handed him a letter address to Mr. George D. Bryson, room 307. But the letter wasn't for him. The previous occupant of room 307 was another man named George D. Bryson.

SET A

A-43	On August 20, 1997, at the age of 59, Dawn Brooke, a British housewife, became the oldest mother to give birth without fertility treatment. The 4-kilo (9-pound) boy was delivered by Caesarian section.
A-44	Bill Roberts (USA) wanted to have his funeral while he was still alive. He even walked ahead of the coffin and its 6 pallbearers to a reception with family and friends. ▪ In 2007, Amir Vehabovic, a 45-year-old man from Bosnia, faked his own death to see how many people would go to his funeral. Only his mother turned up.
A-45	Newlyweds in France are gifted a new chamber pot on their wedding night. After the wedding, before they retire to bed, they must share a dish served in it, typically a mixture of bananas, chocolate, and champagne.
A-46	Scott Damerow (USA) crushed 142 eggs with his head in exactly one minute. ▪ Muhammad Rashid (Pakistan) smashed 35 green coconuts with his head. ▪ Wasantha Soysa (Sri Lanka) broke a stack of 12 concrete blocks with his head.
A-47	Spencer Silver discovered an adhesive that only stuck lightly to surfaces, but he didn't see any use for it. Years later, Art Fry tried that adhesive for a bookmark that would stick to paper without damaging it. Eventually that bookmark became the Post-it Note.
A-48	Brazil has won the World Cup championship five times. ▪ The largest soccer (football) stadium is Rungrado 1st of May Stadium in North Korea. It can seat 114,000 spectators. ▪ Soccer superstar Lionel Messi was the highest paid player in 2020. Between his salary and endorsements, he earned $126 million.

SET A

A-49	The oldest patient operated on was a 118-year-old Punjab woman who was fitted with a pacemaker. ▪ The longest surgery lasted more than four straight days. A team of 20 doctors in Singapore worked in shifts to separate two twins who were conjoined at the head.
A-50	The shortest will ever was written in 1967. It consisted of two words in Czech which mean "All to wife." ▪ The longest will was by Frederica Cook, who died in 1925. Her will was 1,066 pages long and occupied four leather-bound volumes.
A-51	Ziad Fazah, a Liberian-born Lebanese polyglot, claims to speak 59 languages. ▪ According to worldatlas.com the ten most difficult languages for an English speaker are: **1.** Chinese **2.** Arabic **3.** Japanese **4.** Korean **5.** Hindi **6.** Russian **7.** Vietnamese **8.** Turkish **9.** Polish **10.** Thai.
A-52	Spanish painter Salvador Dali (1904–1989) was expelled from art school when he refused to allow his professors to critique his paintings. ▪ Italian dictator Benito Mussolini (1883–1945) was expelled from school when he stabbed a classmate in the buttocks.
A-53	On average, the typical American views about five hours of TV every day. ▪ By the time they graduate high school, a child will have viewed 200,000 acts of violence on television. ▪ Cartoons shown on television display up to 20 violent acts every hour.
A-54	Wilson Mizner (1876–1933) was a writer known for his funny, clever, and amusing remarks. On his deathbed, a priest asked him if he would like to speak to him. Mizner answered, "Why should I talk to you? I've just been talking to your boss."

SET A

A-55	Here are some cures for the hiccups: Stand on your head. ▪ Hold your breath. ▪ Put your fingers in your ears and breathe deeply for a few seconds. ▪ Hold the end of your tongue with your fingers and tug. ▪ Gargle with cold water. ▪ Sing or yell loudly.
A-56	Spanish artist Salvador Dali (1904–1989) once held a party at which every guest came dressed as a bad dream. ▪ Spanish artist Pablo Picasso (1881–1973) was so poor early in his career that he burned some of his drawings to keep warm.
A-57	Fred Hale Sr. (USA) (1890–2004) was issued a driving license at age 104 and drove until it expired on his 108th birthday. ▪ At the age of 77, John Glenn (1921–1916) spent nine days on the space shuttle *Discovery* and became the oldest space traveler.
A-58	Daniel Browning Smith is an American contortionist nicknamed " the Rubber Boy." He's so flexible that he can crawl through an unstrung tennis racquet. ▪ Michel Lotito (1950–2007) was a French entertainer famous for consuming objects made of glass, metal, and rubber. He even dismantled a bicycle and ate it.
A-59	Abraham Lincoln (1809–1865) had a strange dream. In his dream, he heard people sobbing. He walked into a room and noticed a corpse lying on a raised platform. He asked a soldier who the dead person was. The soldier replied, "The president." ▪ Three days, later Lincoln was assassinated.
A-60	Nick Vujicic was born without limbs, but he has feet. ▪ Using his feet, he can type on a computer, throw tennis balls, comb his hair, and shave. ▪ He also swims and skydives. ▪ He starred in the short film *"The Butterfly Circus."* (It'available on YouTube.)

Set B

B-1	Cockroaches appeared about 120 million years before the dinosaurs. • A cockroach found in Peru was the length of a folded wallet. • A cockroach can last for several weeks without its head. It only dies after a couple of weeks because it can't eat or drink.
B-2	The highest town in the world is the gold-mining town of La Rinconada, located in the Peruvian Andes at an elevation of 5,100 meters (16,700 feet) above sea level. It has a population of around 30,000 people.
B-3	Linda Wolfe (USA) has been married 23 times. • Her husbands have included a one-eyed convict, a homeless man, a Mormon preacher, a musician, and a plumber. • One husband lasted just three days. • She married another man three times.
B-4	Do you want to visit Dracula's cemetery? Then you should visit Saint Mary's Church in the seaside town Whitby, England. In the novel, the vampire hides in an abandoned crypt in a church that resembles Saint Mary's. Maybe Dracula is there waiting for you.
B-5	The first written recipe for beer dates back 5,000 years to the Sumerians who lived where modern-day Iraq now stands. • The top five beer-drinking countries are: the Czech Republic, Austria, Germany, Romania, and Poland.
B-6	At age 9, Emily Rosa (USA) had a research paper published in a scientific journal. • At age 10, Vinay Bhat (USA) became a chess Grandmaster. • At age 10, Tatum O'Neal received an Oscar for Best Supporting Actress in the film *Paper Moon*.

SET B

B-7	Mark Kenny (USA) ran 50 meters (164 feet) on his hands in 16 seconds. ▪ Sarah Chapman (UK) walked a distance of 5 kilometers (3 miles) on her hands in an 8-hour period. This was done with periodic rests. ▪ Fan Congcong (China) climbed and descended 40 steps on his hands.
B-8	In 1895, Wilhelm Rontgen (1845–1923) accidentally discovered X Rays. ▪ The first X Ray was of his wife's hand. She wasn't impressed. After seeing the image of her hand, she said, "I have seen my death." ▪ He received the Noble Prize in physics in 1901.
B-9	The largest cemetery in the world is the Wadi al-Salaam Cemetery in Iraq. More than five million people are buried there. ▪ One of the oldest cemeteries is Grotte des Pigeons Cave in Morocco. About 15,000 years ago, the back of the cave was a burial site.
B-10	King Louis VI of France (1081–1137) was so obese that he was given the nickname "Louis the Fat." ▪ Russian czar Ivan IV (1530–1584) was so cruel that he was given the nickname "Ivan the Terrible." He had children thrown into icy rivers and once in a fit of rage killed his own son.
B-11	There are more stars in the universe than grains of sand on all the beaches on Earth. ▪ Our solar system is in a midsize galaxy called the Milky Way, which has over 200 billion stars. ▪ If the Milky Way were shrunk to the size of soccer field, the size of our solar system would be no bigger than a grain of sand.
B-12	There's enough tissue in a pair of human lungs to cover a tennis court. ▪ An adult person inhales and exhales 23,000 times a day. Over a lifetime, the average human breathes enough air to fill 95 huge hot-air balloons.

SET B

B-13	Nadya Suleman, better known as "Octomom," became famous when she gave birth to eight babies in January 2009. ▪ The babies were conceived with the aid of *in vitro* fertilization. ▪ At the time she was a 33-year-old single American mother who already had 6 children.
B-14	Leona Helmsley, a wealthy hotel heiress, left her dog 12 million dollars when she died in 2007. ▪ Luis Carlos da Camara, a wealthy Portuguese aristocrat, left portions of his fortune to 70 persons randomly picked from a Lisbon phone book.
B-15	How many jumping jacks could you do in one minute? Gaber Ali, of Egypt, did 116 jumping jacks in one minute. That's almost two per second. ▪ What's the most you could do? Christian López, of Spain, did 3,744 nonstop jumping jacks in one hour's time.
B-16	The skin of Liew Thow Lin (1930 –2013) of Malaysia had a special property that allowed metal objects weighing as much as 2 kilos (4 pounds) to stick to it. ▪ Hu Qiong of Malaysia has an impenetrable skin. He can withstand a running power drill pressed against his body for one minute without it penetrating his skin.
B-17	Thailand is sometimes known as "the Land of Smiles" because the people of Thailand always seem to be smiling. ▪ Colombia has 18 national holidays. ▪ Australia's first police force was made up of its best-behaved convicts.
B-18	According to a 2020 poll, the 10 happiest countries in the world are: 1. Finland 2. Denmark 3. Switzerland 4. Iceland 5. Norway 6. Netherlands 7. Sweden 8. New Zealand 9. Austria 10. Luxembourg

SET B

B-19	Three inventions you can't live without: **(1)** An alarm clock that wakes you up with a soothing melody and the smell of freshly ground coffee. **(2)** A pillow with a slot for your ear and your glasses. **(3)** A knife that warms butter, making it easier to spread.
B-20	In 1979, a man in Britain tried to defrost his car door lock by blowing on it and got his lips stuck frozen to the metal. He was rescued 20 minutes later. ▪ A burglar in California was arrested after he got stuck in a chimney and had to be rescued.
B-21	Mobster Sam Hunt (1898–1956) was nicknamed "Golf Bag Hunt" because he hid his weapons in a golf bag when he was on a murder mission. ▪ Mafioso Joseph Aiuppa (1907–1997) was nicknamed "Ha Ha" because he never smiled.
B-22	In 1972, a plane carrying Uruguayan rugby players crashed high up in the Andes Mountains. ▪ The 16 survivors had to endure freezing temperatures and eventually had to eat those who had died in the crash. ▪ They were finally rescued 75 days later.
B-23	Jupiter is the biggest planet. Around 11 earths would fit across its diameter. More than 1,300 earths would fit inside of it. ▪ Jupiter has 67 moons. One of them is even bigger than the planet Mercury. Another is considered one of the likeliest places to find life in our solar system.
B-24	Billy and Benny McCrary were the world's heaviest twins. Each of them weighed around 330 kilos (728 pounds). ▪ Despite their size, they lived active lives. They were sensational tag-team wrestlers, drove motorcycles, enjoyed swimming, and flew on airplanes (booking two seats each).

SET B

B-25	Tone Sorensen, of Norway, proposed to her fiancé by using the public address system of a local supermarket while he was shopping for vegetables. ▪ Mateo Martinez popped the question at 20,000 feet just as he and his girlfriend were about to skydive.
B-26	The Tinguian people of the Philippines dress the dead in their best clothes and sit the body on a chair, often placing a lit cigarette in the lips. ▪ The Benguets, also of the Philippines, blindfold their dead and then place them in chairs at the entrance of the home.
B-27	Chocolate was first used in Central America about 2000 B.C. Both the Mayans and the Aztecs made a chocolate drink from the seeds of the cacao tree. ▪ Chocolate bars were only developed in the year 1848 in Bristol, UK, not in Switzerland.
B-28	Edgar Cayce (1877–1945) was an American psychic, known as "the Sleeping Prophet." Working in a trance, he could diagnose the symptoms of a patient he had never seen and then prescribe a cure, often using technical language that he didn't understand when he came out of the trance.
B-29	El Salvador is known as "the Land of Volcanoes." It has more than 20 volcanoes, one of which has erupted 26 times in the last 500 years. ▪ The border between Botswana and Zambia is only 150 meters (492 feet), which makes it the shortest border in the world.
B-30	For a wedding that took place on Halloween, a couple in Canada dressed as Frankenstein and the bride of Frankenstein. ▪ A couple from the United States dressed in black outfits and were wed in a "haunted house" that was full of spider webs, coffins, skeletons, and mummies.

SET B

B-31	If you're famous, getting a divorce can expensive. Here's what some celebrities had to pay their ex-spouses: Kevin Costner ($80 million); Steven Spielberg ($100 million); Michael Jordan ($168 million); Mel Gibson ($425 million); and Jeff Bezos ($68 billion).
B-32	Florence Green (1901-2012), the last veteran of the First World War, died in 2012. Asked what it was like to be 110, she replied, "Not much different to being 109."
B-33	In Germany, after the wedding ceremony, when the newlywed couple leaves the church, friends throw rice on them. It's said that they will have as many children as grains of rice stay in the hair of the bride.
B-34	When the famous physicist Richard Feynman died in 1988, his last words were: "This dying is boring." ▪ Sir Winston Churchill agreed. His last words were: "I'm bored with it all." ▪ The last words of comedian Groucho Marx were: "This is no way to live."
B-35	English actor and comedian Ken Dodd (1927–2018) once told jokes continuously for three and a half hours. During that time, he told 1,500 jokes. ▪ British-American actor and comedian Bob Hope (1903–2003) had a collection of about 500,000 jokes.
B-36	Gérard de Nerval (1808–1855), a poet and author from France, had a pet lobster. He would attach a blue silk ribbon to it and take the live lobster for a walk around the streets of Paris.
B-37	Guillem de Cabestany, a 12th century troubadour, was killed by a jealous husband, who then had his heart cooked and served to his unfaithful wife.

SET B

B-38	A tradition shared by Latin America and Poland allows guests a chance to dance with the bride, but for a price. • Guests have to pay to dance with the bride. • The money is collected by the maid of honor and is used to pay for the couple's honeymoon.
B-39	How many pancakes do you think you could eat in 8 minutes? The record is 113. • How many waffles could you eat in 10 minutes? The record is 29.
B-40	Identical twins Jim Springer and Jim Lewis were separated at birth. Both were adopted and renamed James. • Both had a dog named Toy. • Both became policemen. • And both had wives named Linda, who they later divorced for women named Betty.
B-41	Ashrita Furman somersaulted continuously for 19 kilometers (12 miles). • Suresh Joachim (Canada, born in Sri Lanka) crawled 56 kilometers (35 miles) by completing laps around the Queen Victoria Building in Australia.
B-42	What do Napoleon, Mark Twain, and George Washington have in common? They were all redheads. • What do Greenland, New Guinea, and Borneo have in common? They are the three largest islands in the world.
B-43	A blink takes just 140th of a second. • On the average, a person blinks 15-20 times per minute. About 1,200 times an hour, 28,800 times a day, and over 10 million times in a year. • Men blink twice as often as women.
B-44	In 2014, Bill Standley, from the state of Ohio, was buried seated on his Harley Davidson motorcycle. • In 1998, Rose Martin, from the state of Massachusetts, was buried seated in her 1962 sports car.

SET B

B-45	The earliest frogs emerged some 150 million years ago. • The world's smallest frog is found in Papua New Guinea. It's around the size of a housefly. • The world's biggest frog is bigger than the world's smallest antelope.
B-46	Lightning strikes the earth 8.6 million times a day or about 100 times a second. • In 1939, 835 sheep were killed by a lightning bolt in the American state of Utah. • A bolt of lightning can have a temperature five times hotter than the surface of the sun.
B-47	The tallest woman ever was Zeng Jinlian of China (1964–1982). She was 2.46 meters (8 feet 1 inch) tall. That's taller than the front door of a house. • Her parents were short, shorter than 1.6 meters (5 feet 2 inches) tall.
B-48	It takes 17 muscles to smile and 43 to frown. • To say a single word, about 100 muscles in the chest, neck, jaw, tongue, and lips must work together. • To take a single step forward, 200 muscles must work in unison.
B-49	The average four-year-old child asks 450 questions a day. • When Einstein was two and a half years old, he was presented to his new baby sister. Thinking she was a toy, he asked, "Where are its wheels?"
B-50	A can of Coke has about 9 teaspoons of sugar. • A 30-year-old woman died after drinking 7 liters (2 gallons) of Coke daily for years. An autopsy revealed that Coke had ruined her liver and her heart, and that all of her teeth were rotten.

SET B

B-51	In 1930, Charles Creighton and James Hargis drove their 1929 Ford Roadster from New York City to Los Angeles, a distance of 5,380 kilometers (3,340 miles). But the most amazing thing is that they drove the whole way in reverse.
B-52	Brazilian surfer Maya Gabeira set a record for the largest wave surfed by a female. The wave was 22.4 meters (73 feet) tall. That's as tall as a 7-story building. ▪ In 1907, Irish-Hawaiian George Freeth (1883–1919) introduced surfing to California.
B-53	The largest hotel in the world is the First World Hotel in Malaysia with a total of 7,351 rooms. ▪ The most expensive hotel room is the Empathy Suite in the Palms Casino Resort in Las Vegas. The room costs $100,000 per night with a minimum two-night stay.
B-54	Actress Emma Roberts won't walk under ladders. ▪ Actress Megan Fox believes she won't die in a plane crash as long as she's listening to Britney Spears on her iPhone. ▪ Singer Taylor Swift writes the number 13 on her hand before every performance.
B-55	The chances you will be struck by lightning are about 1 in 2 million. ▪ Roy Sullivan (1912–1983), a ranger in a state park in Virginia, was a "human lightning rod." Over a period of 35 years, he survived being struck by lightning seven times.
B-56	Judo was created in Japan in 1882 by Jigoro Kano as a physical, mental, and moral exercise. ▪ World champion boxer Muhammad Ali (1942–2016) took up boxing as a boy so he could clobber a thief who stole his bicycle.

SET B

B-57	Larry Walters attached 45 weather balloons to his lawn chair and filled them with helium. When his friends cut the cord securing the chair, Larry, seated in his chair, rose to 4,900 meters (16,000 feet), earning him the nickname "Lawn Chair Larry."
B-58	The oldest man to ascend Everest is Yuichiro Miura (Japan), who reached the summit at the age of 80 years. ▪ At age 85, Canadian Ed Whitlock became the oldest person to run a marathon in less than four hours.
B-59	The shortest war in history was between Great Britain and Zanzibar in 1896. It lasted just 45 minutes. ▪ China is estimated to have an army of 2,035,000 soldiers. ▪ Iceland doesn't have an army. It just has 130 active paramilitaries.
B-60	A museum in Germany once displayed a "painting" that was a totally blank canvas with a frame. ▪ A painting by Henri Matisse (1869–1954) spent 47 days hanging upside down in the Museum of Modern Art in New York City, unnoticed by 116,000 viewers.
B-61	A favorite meal of Charles Darwin was armadillo. ▪ For his breakfast, Abraham Lincoln would often have apples, bacon, and coffee. ▪ Mozart loved a plate of sauerkraut topped with liver dumplings. ▪ Beethoven's favorite dish was mac and cheese.
B-62	Robert Briggs was hiking in the California wilderness when he was suddenly attacked by a mountain lion. ▪ A black bear nearby came to his rescue, driving the mountain lion away. ▪ The bear then lowered down over Briggs, looked him in the eyes, and walked off.

Set C

C-1	The heart of a blue whale is as large as a small car. ▪ Its tongue weighs as much as an elephant, and almost 50 people could stand on it. ▪ A blue whale eats around 4 tons of krill (tiny sea creatures) a day. That's equal to the weight of 2 hippopotamuses.
C-2	The average person who lives to be 75 will have spent six years dreaming. The average person forgets 90% of their dreams. The colder the room you sleep in, the higher the chances are that you'll have a bad dream.
C-3	Darren McWalters and Katie Hodgson were married standing on top of the wings of two planes flying 300 meters (1,000 feet) above the ground. ▪ The groom stood on the top of the wing of one biplane, while his bride, in her full bridal gown, was on the wing of another plane. ▪ The minister was on top of a third plane.
C-4	When England's Sir Walter Raleigh was beheaded in 1618, his wife buried his body but kept his embalmed head in a bag for the last 30 years of her life. ▪ Mary Shelley, author of the book *Frankenstein*, kept the heart of her dead husband in her desk.
C-5	Oscar Wilde (1854–1900) was a celebrated Irish poet and playwright noted for his wit. His last words were: "Either that wallpaper goes, or I do" ▪ When American comedian and actor Bob Hope (1903–2003) was on his deathbed, his wife asked him where he wanted to be buried. His answer: "Surprise me."
C-6	How many hot dogs in a bun do you think you could eat in ten minutes? The world record is 75. ▪ How many hamburgers do you think you could eat in three minutes? The world record is 12.

SET C

C-7	There are more McDonald's restaurants in the United States than hospitals. ▪ Actors Rachel McAdams and James Franco; singers Seal, Pink, and Shania Twain; and Amazon founder Jeff Bezos all worked at McDonald's when they were young.
C-8	In 2001, 10-year-old Laura Buxton released a balloon from her backyard with her name and address written on it. ▪ The recipient ended up being another 10-year-old girl also named Laura Buxton. ▪ To make matters crazier, they both owned black Labrador dogs and gray rabbits, were the same height, and had brown hair.
C-9	According to a 2020 poll, the 10 happiest cities in the world are: **1.** Helsinki **2.** Aarhus, Denmark **3.** Wellington, New Zealand **4.** Zurich **5.** Copenhagen **6.** Bergen, Norway **7.** Oslo, Norway **8.** Tel Aviv **9.** Stockholm **10.** Brisbane, Australia
C-10	The fragrance of apples and bananas can help a person to lose weight. ▪ You can lose 150 calories per hour by hitting your head against the wall. ▪ Jon Minnoch (USA) spent 16 months in the hospital during which time he lost 419 kilos (924 pounds).
C-11	Albert Einstein (1879–1955) bought sets of identical clothes to avoid wasting time having to match clothing every day. ▪ John Paul Getty (1892–1976), one of the richest men who ever lived, had a pay telephone in one of his mansions for his guests to use.
C-12	There's a psychological disorder known as the Stendhal Syndrome in which people experience heart palpitations and dizziness when viewing great works of art. ▪ People who have Foreign Accent Syndrome adopt a foreign accent, often after having suffered a stroke.

SET C

C-13	In Finland, traffic fines are calculated according to the offender's income. ▪ In early 2004, Jussi Salonoja, the heir to a meatpacking empire, was caught driving double the speed limit. ▪ He had to pay a fine equal to $216,900.
C-14	In 1992, a premedical student at Adelphi University in New York was arrested for stealing half of a human head from the anatomy lab. ▪ In Texas, a pastor of the First Missionary Baptist Church stole the pulpit after the church had voted to replace him.
C-15	The planet Mars is named after the Roman god of war. It's about half the size of the earth. ▪ If you want to lose weight you should move to Mars. If you weigh 70 kilos (150 pounds) on Earth, you would only weigh 26 kilos (57 pounds) on Mars.
C-16	In their lifetime, the average human will grow 28 meters (92 feet) of fingernails; spend a total of three years going to the bathroom; produce 40,000 liters (10,500 gallons) of urine; blink 415 million times; and grow 950 kilometers (590 miles) of hair their head.
C-17	The lightest adult ever was Lucia Zarate, a Mexican entertainer who performed in circus sideshows. ▪ At the age of 17, she weighed just 2.1 kilos (4.7 pounds). That's about the same as a common building brick or two pineapples. ▪ She died from cold temperatures when her train got stranded in a snowstorm.
C-18	In Mauritania, a country in Africa, obesity in women is seen as desirable. So, brides in Mauritania do all they can to put on weight before the wedding. ▪ Brides get married in a beautifully embroidered black robe. ▪ The grooms dress in white.

SET C

C-19	French fries aren't from France; they come from Belgium. ▪ Apple pie isn't an American dish; it actually originated in medieval England. ▪ Fortune cookies aren't from China; they originated in a bakery in the United States in the early 1900s. ▪ Pasta isn't from Italy; it originated in China long before Italy knew of it.
C-20	How far do you think you could throw a standard building brick that weighs 2.3 kilos (5 pounds)? Geoffrey Capes of England, twice winner of the title of The World's Strongest Man, threw a brick 44 meters (146 feet). That's the length of three city buses.
C-21	Homes in Paraguay don't have doorbells—people clap at the front gate. ▪ The earliest evidence of wine has been found in Georgia, where 8,000-year-old wine jars have been found. ▪ The tradition of painting Easter eggs first began in Ukraine.
C-22	In German there's a word to describe "a present that a man brings to his wife to apologize for being out late." ▪ In Gaelic there's a word which means "the kind of friend who only drops in at mealtimes."
C-23	Actress Jennifer Aniston is afraid of flying. ▪ Actors Daniel Radcliffe and Johnny Depp are afraid of clowns. ▪ Singer Sheryl Crow is afraid of heights. ▪ Actress Nicole Kidman is afraid of butterflies. ▪ Caesar, Shakespeare, and Hitler were afraid of cats.
C-24	The largest dinosaur was discovered in Argentina in 1986. ▪ It measured 36 meters (120 feet) from head to tail. That's longer than two city buses. ▪ It was taller than a 6-story building and weighed more than 30 elephants.

SET C

C-25	Sunlight takes 8 minutes to reach earth; 12 minutes to reach Mars; 43 minutes to reach Jupiter; over 5 hours to reach Pluto; 4 years to reach the nearest star (Alpha Centauri); and 2.5 million years to reach the nearest major galaxy (Andromeda).
C-26	A man named Reed Harris hid the engagement ring for his prospective fiancée in a milkshake. ▪ American inventor Thomas Edison proposed to his future wife by tapping out his proposal in Morse code in the palm of her hand.
C-27	Identical twins Ann and Claire Recht (USA) are the world's tallest female twins. ▪ They're 2 meters (6 feet 7 inches) tall. That's about the same height as the front door of a house. ▪ Reaching up, they can easily touch the ceiling without standing on their toes.
C-28	A man in the state of Maine (USA) divorced his wife because she wore earplugs whenever his mother came to visit. ▪ A man in the state of Idaho (USA) filed for divorce because his wife dressed up as a ghost and tried to scare his elderly mother out of the house.
C-29	American chemist Fred Baur created the Pringles potato chip can. When he died, he was cremated, and his ashes were buried in a Pringles can. ▪ In his will, Bill Johnson (USA) asked that his ashes be placed in two dozen firework shells and set off in the sky.
C-30	In Italy, you can visit the Church of the Dead. ▪ It houses over a dozen mummies that stand guard inside the church. ▪ These mummies have been standing in their upright glass-covered cases looking out at visitors since the early 19th century.

SET C

C-31	At 82, Ivy Baldwin (1866–1953) became the oldest tightrope walker when he crossed a canyon in the state of Colorado on a 97-meter (320-foot) wire 38 meters (125 feet) above the canyon floor. ▪ The youngest tightrope walker was a three-year-old girl in China who walked on a tightrope over nine Siberian tigers.
C-32	Over a period of 10 years, Emilio Scotto (Argentina) rode his motorcycle through 279 countries, travelling a total of 735,000 kilometers (457,000 miles). He went through 13 passports. He met with the Pope, and in Africa he was arrested as a suspected spy.
C-33	The potato chip was invented in 1853 by George Speck (1824–1914), a chef at a resort in New York. When a customer complained that the French-fried potatoes were too thick, he sliced and fried some that were too thin to eat with a fork, and potato chips were born.
C-34	What do Napoleon, Churchill, Charles Dickens, Thomas Edison, Benjamin Franklin, and Van Gogh have in common? They were all insomniacs. ▪ What do Abraham Lincoln, Mussolini, and George Washington have in common? They were all snorers.
C-35	The most expensive painting ever is *Salvator Mundi*, Leonardo da Vinci's depiction of Jesus Christ holding a crystal orb. It sold for $450 million. ▪ Paintings of animals and handprints in the El Castillo cave in Cantabria, Spain, are at least 40,800 years old.
C-36	Vernon Kruger (South Africa) stayed in a barrel at the top of a 21-meter (70-foot) pole for 67 days. ▪ Swami Maujgiri Maharij (India) stood up continuously for 17 years, from 1955 to 1973, while doing penance. He slept leaning against a plank.

SET C

C-37	In 1883, Krakatoa, a volcano in Indonesia, erupted with a force that was about 10,000 times more powerful than the atomic bomb that destroyed Hiroshima. The explosion was heard 4,500 kilometers (2,800 miles) away, and over 36,000 people perished.
C-38	Kin Narita and Gin Kanie were born in Japan in 1892. ▪ They hold the record for the greatest age reached by twins, 107 years and 175 days. ▪ At the age of 100 they recorded a rap record which made the pop charts in Japan.
C-39	In Scotland, in the days prior to a marriage, the bride and groom are captured by friends, covered in food and sticky substances, and then driven around in an open-backed truck while friends and family bang pots and pans.
C-40	William Harvey (1578–1657), the 17th century English doctor who discovered how blood circulates, believed coffee was "the source of happiness and wit." ▪ King Frederick the Great (1712–1786), of Prussia, drank coffee brewed with champagne instead of water.
C-41	A South Korean woman failed her driving test 771 times. ▪ Once a 75-year-old male driver in Texas received 10 traffic tickets, drove on the wrong side of the road 4 times, and caused 6 accidents—all within 20 minutes.
C-42	The Chihuahua, the world's smallest dog, is named after a state in Mexico. ▪ The people in Ghana dress in brightly colored clothing, preferably made of silk. ▪ India gave the world yoga, chess, and herbal shampoo.

SET C

C-43	George Washington once borrowed a book and forgot to return it. Over 220 years later it was found and returned to the library. The library waved the $300,000 late fee. ▪ A woman in the USA paid an overdue book fine for a book her mother had checked out 47 years earlier. The fine, at two cents a day, came to $345.
C-44	In the 1970s, a Finnish architect designed houses shaped like flying saucers. ▪ In Pennsylvania, there's a house built in the form of a shoe. ▪ Bangkok has a high-rise building that resembles an elephant. ▪ Seoul Korea has a tower built in the form of a hashtag.
C-45	There are about 1,900 volcanoes on earth that are considered active, likely to erupt again. ▪ The Stromboli volcano in Italy is currently one of the most active volcanoes on Earth. It's been erupting almost continuously since 1932.
C-46	During their lifetime, the average person spends 38 days brushing their teeth. ▪ The first toothbrushes were tree twigs with the tips chewed to spread the fibers. ▪ The ancient Romans used a mixture of goat milk and urine to keep their teeth white.
C-47	Canadian millionaire Charles Millar (1854–1926) left nine million dollars to be awarded to the Canadian woman giving birth to the most babies in the ten years following his death. ▪ He also left a home in Jamaica to three men who he knew hated each other.
C-48	In South Korea, you can compress the cremated remains of a relative into colorful, shiny blue, green, pink, or black beads. The beads are kept in jars and even used as home decorations, as a decorative way to keep the deceased nearby.

SET C

C-49	At the age of 92 and with two artificial knees, Herb Tanner made a solo parachute jump. ▪ Skydiver Klint Freemantle's main and back-up parachutes failed to open. He landed in a pond and then walked out with just a small cut over his left eye.
C-50	Ashrita Furman (USA) walked for nearly 14 kilometers (9 miles) balancing a pool cue (stick) on his finger. ▪ Christian Roberto Rodríguez (Spain) balanced a broom on his nose for one hour and 30 minutes. ▪ Jay Rawlings (UK) balanced 56 rolls of toilet paper on his head.
C-51	The first Ferris wheel was designed and built by George Ferris Junior (1859–1896) for the 1893 World's Fair in Chicago. It was as tall as a 26-story building. ▪ The world's tallest Ferris wheel is the Dubai Eye in Dubai. It's as tall as a 70-story building.
C-52	The most expensive omelet is the Zillion Dollar Lobster Frittata served at the Parker Meridien Hotel in New York. For $2,000 you get an omelet made with an entire large lobster and a large amount of caviar. ▪ In 1955, the first McDonald's hamburgers cost only 15 cents.
C-53	Diamond Jim Brady (1856–1917) loved expensive jewelry and eating. ▪ For dinner he would eat steaks, a few dozen oysters, a dozen crabs, half a dozen lobsters, and soup. ▪ For dessert he always had an enormous quantity of bonbons followed by pastries.
C-54	During his lifetime, Van Gogh (1853–1890) sold only one painting, and this was to a friend. ▪ Charles Schulz (1922–2000), creator of the Peanuts comic strip, had every cartoon he submitted for his high school yearbook rejected.

SET C

C-55	Alex Mullen (USA) has a super memory. ▪ He can accurately recall airline departure and arrival locations, as well as the routes and times of 50 flights. ▪ He can memorize the order of a deck of cards flashed onscreen at two cards per second.
C-56	In a Paris bookstore, American novelist Anne Parrish (1888–1957) came upon a book that had been one of her childhood favorites. Inside was the inscription "This book belongs to Anne Parrish." Incredibly, it was Anne's very own childhood book.
C-57	Russian Oxana Seroshtan walked 15 meters (49 feet) on a tightrope in high heels. ▪ Maurizio Zavatta (Italy) walked on a tightrope 212 meters (696 feet) high while blindfolded. He also ran 100 meters (330 feet) backwards on a tightrope in just over one minute.
C-58	Jeane Dixon (1904–1997) was an American psychic and astrologer. She predicted the assassination of President John Kennedy and the launch of the world's first satellite. Just before she died, she predicted that the hope of humankind would be found in the East.
C-59	In 1922 in England, 24-year-old Theresa Vaughn was charged with bigamy. In five years, she had accumulated 62 husbands, without ever having been divorced or widowed.
C-60	At the age of 11, Stephanie Taylor (USA) founded the nonprofit organization Vest-A-Dog that raises money to buy bulletproof vests for police dogs. ▪ At age 11, Victoria Van Meter (1982–2008) became the youngest girl to pilot a plane across the United States.
C-61	Jose Garcia, of Cordoba, Mexico, became a father and a great grandfather on the same day.

Set D

D-1	If you were on a space shuttle travelling 20,000 kilometers (12,400 miles) per hour, it would take around 165 thousand years to reach the closest star in our galaxy, Proxima Centauri, which is just over four light years away.
D-2	If you like lots of people around you, then surely Greenland isn't the place for you. It's the least densely populated place on Earth. There are only 56,000 people in the whole country, while Mexico, a country of about the same size, has over 125 million people.
D-3	By 60 years of age, 60% of men and 40% of women will snore. ▪ It can be as loud as a group of people talking (60 decibels); a vacuum cleaner (75 decibels); a kitchen blender (85 decibels); and even a chainsaw (110 decibels).
D-4	The shortest man ever was Chandra Bahadur Dangi (1939–2015) from Nepal. He was 54 centimeters (1 foot 9 inches) tall. About the same size as six stacked cans of baked beans. He was shorter than an average six-month-old child.
D-5	For their wedding in 1992, Evan Barton and his bride both wore a full suit of armor. ▪ When John and Lynn Lauersdorf met, they were working for a tree-care company. So naturally they were married while hanging from the branches of a tree.
D-6	The Ga people of Ghana use coffins that symbolize the life of the dead person. ▪ The coffin of a fisherman might be in the shape of a giant fish, while a pilot might have his coffin in the shape of an airplane. ▪ Coffins also take the shape of animals, fruits, and other items of daily life.

SET D

D-7	Zeng Jia, a 22-year-old student from China, decided to stage her own funeral. ▪ There were flowers and a crowd of mourners. ▪ She spent an hour playing dead in a coffin. ▪ Then she jumped out and delivered a eulogy in her own honor.
D-8	How many bananas do you think you could peel and eat in one minute? The record is 8. ▪ In 2012, Ashrita Furman (USA) was able to peel and eat 6 hard-boiled eggs in only one minute. That's an average of one egg every 10 seconds.
D-9	In 1979, Ted Coombs (USA) traveled from Los Angeles, California, to New York City and back on roller skates, about 8,400 kilometers (5,200 miles). ▪ John Slater walked from Scotland to Lands End, England, in his bare feet, about 900 kilometers (570 miles).
D-10	In parts of Mexico, grasshoppers fried in garlic and lemon are a favorite food ▪ Duck eggs cooked just before they are ready to hatch are regarded as a delicacy in the Philippines. ▪ The Bantu tribes of Africa eat termites cooked in vegetable oil and salt.
D-11	In the 1930s, as Joseph Figlock was walking down the street, a baby from a high window fell and landed on to him. Both Figlock and the baby were unharmed. ▪ A year later, the very same baby fell from the very same window once again onto Figlock as he was again passing underneath. They again both survived the event.
D-12	At age 100, Bo Gilbert, of Birmingham, England, became a fashion model when she was featured in the British Vogue magazine's 100th anniversary edition. ▪ At the age of 114, Jeanne Louise Calment (France, 1875–1997) acted in the film *Vincent and Me*.

SET D

D-13	Frenchman Sylvain Dornon (1858–1900) performed folk dances on stilts. He climbed the 674 steps up to the second floor of the Eiffel Tower on stilts. In 1891, he stilt-walked from Paris to Moscow in 58 days. ▪ Ashrita Furman (USA) ran 8 kilometers (5 miles) on stilts in just under 40 minutes.
D-14	In Croatia, there's a Museum of Broken Relationships in which people deposit mementos of their lost loves. ▪ The local dish of Siri Lanka is rice and curry, which they eat by scooping it up with their right hand.
D-15	What do Charles Dickens, Thomas Edison, and Claude Monet have in common? They never graduated from grade school. ▪ What do bulldogs, Saint Bernards, Irish setters, and Great Danes have in common? They're the breeds of dogs that bark the least.
D-16	In German, there's a word meaning "the weight you put on from eating too much when feeling sorry for yourself." ▪ In Portuguese, there's a word that means "the act of romantically running one's fingers through someone's hair."
D-17	Singer Ariana Grande would eat chocolate donuts before auditions for good luck. ▪ Picasso (1881–1973) wouldn't throw away his fingernail clippings for fear it would mean losing part of his "essence." ▪ Author Truman Capote (1924–1984) refused to fly on a plane if more than two nuns were aboard.
D-18	Carol Vaughn has a collection of more than 5,000 bars of soap from all over the world. ▪ Jean Vernetti has over 11,000 Do Not Disturb signs from hotels across the globe. ▪ Jackie Miley has 7,106 unique teddy bears. ▪ Bettina Dorfman owns 6,025 Barbie dolls.

SET D

D-19	Michael Jordan (USA), one the best basketball players ever, was cut from his high school basketball team. ▪ Before J. K. Rowling created Harry Potter, she was nearly penniless, severely depressed, and divorced, trying to raise a child on her own.
D-20	The Hurried-Child Syndrome is the neurotic result of parents pushing their children to excel academically while overscheduling their free time with many extracurricular activities. ▪ Anglolalia is an uncontrollable urge to affect a British accent.
D-21	A man from Cairo, Egypt, trained camels to wash windows by coating the glass with sugar and water. ▪ A large camel can drink around 30 gallons (113 liters) of water in just 13 minutes. That's equal to the gas tanks of two compact cars.
D-22	Mercury is now the smallest planet in the solar system (Pluto is no longer considered a planet). It's only slightly bigger than our moon. ▪ Saturn and Jupiter each have a moon that's bigger than Mercury. ▪ Mercury rotate so very slowly that one day on the planet is actually longer than one year on the planet.
D-23	The average 75-year-old person has spent 220,000 hours sleeping. That's equal to about 25 years of their life. ▪ Most people take 10 to 20 minutes to fall asleep once they have climbed into bed. ▪ You would die quicker from a total lack of sleep than from hunger.
D-24	Paolina and Ake Viking were married as a result of Paolina's father picking up a bottle with a message inside of it off the coast of Sicily. The message asked any pretty girl to write. Paolina wrote back, and she and Ake eventually met and married.

SET D

D-25	A tradition of the Tidong tribe of Malaysia is that for three days after the wedding the bride and groom may not go to the bathroom. It's believed that this will show a strong commitment and a strong will to make their marriage as perfect as they can.
D-26	In the 17th century, people added butter to their coffee. ▪ Black ivory coffee from Thailand is the most expensive coffee in the world. It's made from beans that have been collected from elephant poop. It sells for as much as $50 a cup.
D-27	"Uncle Billy Hooper"(USA) could stand on his head at the age of eighty-six. ▪ Suresh Joachim (born in Sri Lanka) stood on one foot for 76 hours. ▪ Chinese Acrobat Li Longlong managed to climb 36 stairs without touching the steps with anything but his head.
D-28	German composer Christoph Gluck (1714–1787) refused to sleep in his room one night after seeing a ghost-like figure enter it. The next morning, he found that the ceiling had collapsed on his bed and would have killed him if he had been lying in it.
D-29	In 2019, the 10 most livable cities were: 1. Vienna, Austria 2. Melbourne, Australia 3. Sydney, Australia 4. Osaka, Japan 5. Calgary, Canada 6. Vancouver, Canada 7. Tokyo, Japan 8. Toronto, Canada 9. Copenhagen, Denmark 10 Adelaide, Australia
D-30	Finland gave us the sauna, the phone app Angry Birds, the heart-rate monitor, the rescue toboggan, ice skates, and the Linux operating system. ▪ Brazil is the only country in South America that speaks Portuguese.

SET D

D-31	The average woman smiles 62 times a day, while the average man smiles about 8 times a day. • Men are less likely to seek regular medical checkups. • Women worry more than men. • Men tolerate sleep deprivation better than women do. When women don't get enough sleep, they suffer mentally and physically.
D-32	The tallest roller coaster is Kingda Ka (USA). At its top, it's as high as a 45-story building. • The fastest roller coaster is Formula Rossa in the city of Abu Dhabi. It reaches 100 km/h (60 mph) in just 2 seconds. It reaches a top speed of 240 km/h (149.1 mph).
D-33	The West Edmond Mall in Canada has 800 stores; a haunted house; an indoor triple-loop roller coaster; a miniature golf course; an indoor water park; night clubs; an indoor lake containing live sea lions; a petting zoo; a hotel; cinemas; and much more.
D-34	The Palace of the Sultan of Brunei has over 1,700 rooms, 257 toilets, and a garage for 110 cars. • Buckingham Palace has 775 rooms, including 188 staff bedrooms, 92 offices, and 78 bathrooms. • The White House Residence has 132 rooms and 35 bathrooms.
D-35	In the United States, March 13th is National Blame It on Somebody Else Day. • In January of 1999, 2,000 people in Bombay celebrated World Laughter Day by laughing out loud in a city park. • In the United States, May 10th is Clean Up Your Room Day.
D-36	When actor-comedian Groucho Marx (1890–1977) had insomnia, he would telephone people in the middle of the night and insult them. • US president Theodore Roosevelt (1858–1919) had a cure for his insomnia: a shot of cognac in a glass of milk.

SET D

D-37	One of the first examples of false advertising occurred over a thousand years ago when Viking explorer Erik the Red gave the name Greenland to a barren, ice-covered island in the hopes of attracting potential settlers.
D-38	The sticky tongue of the chameleon extends up to 1½ times its body length to capture an insect and zip it into its mouth, all in less than a second. ▪ The okapi, an animal found in central Africa, has a tongue that's 45 centimeters (18 inches) long, which it uses to wash its eyelids.
D-39	In A.D. 79, the Italian town of Pompeii was destroyed and buried in ash by a volcano called Mount Vesuvius. ▪ The ash preserved many buildings, artwork, and even the forms of bodies. ▪ Pompeii was basically lost and forgotten until it was rediscovered in 1748.
D-40	If allowed to grow for their whole lifetime, the length of someone's hair would be about 725 kilometers (450 miles) long. ▪ The world's longest hair belongs to a Chinese woman (Xie Qiuping). In 2004, her hair was 5.6 meters (18 feet) long.
D-41	Maggie Kuhn (1905–1995) was the founder of the Gray Panthers, a movement whose purpose was to encourage activism by and in support of older people. ▪ She was frequently asked why she wasn't married. Her standard response was: "sheer luck."
D-42	A deaf man in South Carolina (USA) filed for divorce because his wife was always nagging him in sign language. ▪ A woman in Colorado (USA) divorced her husband because he forced her to hide herself whenever they drove past his girlfriend's house.

SET D

D-43	At the wedding reception of newlywed Swedish couples, if the groom leaves the room, the male guests are permitted to kiss the bride. Similarly, if the bride leaves the party, female guests get to kiss the groom.
D-44	Just outside of Anchorage, Alaska, there's a unique cemetery with graves covered by spirit houses. ▪ First a blanket is placed over the grave. ▪ Then, 40 days later, a colorful house is built to protect their spirit and to represent the person that was laid to rest there.
D-45	Sobrino de Botín, located in Madrid, is the oldest continuously operating restaurant in the world. ▪ It has been serving meals since 1725, nearly 300 years. ▪ Its most famous dish is *cochinillo asado* (roast piglet).
D-46	Backpacker Babis Bizas (Greece) has visited all 195 countries in the world, not just once but twice. ▪ The youngest person to visit every country is Lexie Alford (USA) who accomplished this before she was 22 years old.
D-47	At the age of 14, Romanian gymnast Nadia Comaneci became the first athlete in Olympic history to achieve a perfect 10. ▪ At age 91, German gymnast Johanna Quaas was still doing cartwheels, headstands, and working the parallel bars.
D-48	Brent Fraser (USA) caught a grape in his mouth that was dropped from a height of 30 meters (101 feet). ▪ Pavol Durdik (Slovakia) tossed a grape in the air and caught it in his mouth 162 times in a row. ▪ Ashrita Furman (USA) caught 86 grapes in his mouth in one minute.

SET D

D-49	In 2006, The Rolling Stones gave a free concert on Rio de Janeiro's famous Copacabana Beach for over 1.5 million fans. ▪ Every concert, lead singer Mick Jagger struts, stomps, and staggers an estimated 12 miles. To keep in shape, he follows a fitness regimen that includes jogging, kickboxing, yoga, and even ballet.
D-50	An 80-year-old South African man was presumed dead and put in a refrigerator in a morgue. Twenty-one hours later, the dead man woke up and started screaming, terrifying the morgue staff, who thought the man was a ghost and called the police.
D-51	It's never too late. When they were married in in 2015, George Kirby was exactly 103 years old (it was his birthday) and Doreen Luckie was 91 years and 280 days.
D-52	William Cobb (1613–1665), of England, was the father of 2 priests and 4 nuns. ▪ Doctor Jahial Parmly (USA) was the brother of 3 dentists and the uncle, brother-in-law, and cousin of 14 dentists.
D-53	English surgeon Joseph Henry Green (1791–1863) pointed to his chest and said, "Congestion." He then checked his own pulse, looked up, and uttered his last word: "Stopped."
D-54	Japan has a baby crying competition. The first baby to cry is the winner. ▪ Australia has Australia Day cockroach races. ▪ Northern England has a toe wrestling competition. ▪ Colorado (USA) is home to the annual Emma Crawford Coffin Race.
D-55	German author Heinrich Heine (1797–1856) left his entire estate to his wife on the condition that she remarry. Allegedly he said, "At least there will be one man to regret my death."

SET D

D-56	A dog named Chi Chi was sitting with his owners on a beach. He suddenly sprang up and began barking. He had spotted an elderly couple who had been carried out to sea by a large wave. His barks alerted his owners, and they were able to save the couple.
D-57	David "the Bullet" Smith Jr. is a human cannonball. ▪ He gets ejected out of specially designed compressed-air cannons and lands in a net at the predicted landing point. ▪ He has reached the height of a 9-story building and has flown almost 60 meters (195 feet).
D-58	Hadji Ali (1892–1937) was a performing artist in the early 1900s. For his act, he would swallow watermelon seeds, jewels, coins, and other small objects. Then he would regurgitate specific items as requested by the audience.
D-59	Veronica Seider (Germany) has incredible vision. She can identify people from 1.6 kilometers (1 mile) away. ▪ Arthur Lintgen (USA) can look at the grooves of LP phonograph records and identify the piece of classical music, but only if it's either by or after Beethoven.
D-60	The largest toothpick sculpture is an alligator made by Michael Smith (Port Allen, USA). This sculpture contains over 3 million toothpicks, is 4.5 meters (15 feet) long, and weighs 132 kilos (292 pounds). ▪ Eskimos used walrus whiskers as toothpicks.
D-61	The beard of Hans Langseth, born in Norway in 1846, measured 5.33 meters (17 feet 6 inches) at the time of his death. ▪ The longest mustache belongs to Ram Singh Chauhan (India). In 2010, it was measured at 4.29 meters (14 feet).

Set E

E-1	Cat owners are 30% less likely to suffer a heart attack. Cats were so sacred in ancient Egypt that they were mummified. ▪ The heaviest recorded cat is a cat from Australia. It weighed 21 kilos (46 pounds). About the same as a five-year-old child.
E-2	The moon is a dusty ball of rock roughly a quarter of the size of the earth. ▪ In 1969, the first astronauts from Earth set foot on the moon. It took them 4 days 6 hours and 45 minutes to reach it. The first astronauts were Neil Armstrong (1930–2012) and Buzz Aldrin (born 1930).
E-3	The human brain weighs around 1.5 kilos (about 3 pounds) and has a texture like firm tofu. ▪ It contains 100 billion neurons. ▪ A single human brain generates more electrical impulses in a day than all the telephones of the world combined.
E-4	Donna Griffiths (UK) had a sneezing fit that lasted 976 days. She sneezed an estimated one million times in the first 365 days. ▪ An American named Charles Osborne hiccupped continuously for 68 years, for an estimated 430 million hiccups.
E-5	Turkish bridegrooms were once required to make a promise during their wedding ceremonies to always provide their new wives with coffee. If they failed to do so, it was grounds for divorce.
E-6	In the United States, you can have a green or natural burial. The body is neither cremated nor embalmed. It's simply placed in a biodegradable coffin. The goal is complete decomposition of the body and its natural return to the soil.

SET E

E-7	The last words of murderer Gary Gilmore before his execution in 1976 were: "Let's do it." Some 12 years later these words inspired the "Just do it" slogan of the Nike shoe ads. ▪ The last words of murderer Jimmy Glass were: "I'd rather be fishing."
E-8	Since 1972, Donald Gorske (USA) has eaten a lot of McDonalds Big Mac burgers. Can you guess how many? On May 4th, 2018 he ate his 30,000th Big Mac. He typically eats 14 Big Macs each week, purchasing them in bulk and microwaving them at home.
E-9	Aneta Florczyk, born in Poland in 1982, has held the title of the World's Strongest Woman several times. In one competition, she lifted 12 adult men over her head in two minutes. ▪ Strongwoman Heini Koivuniemi, of Finland, threw a 12-kilo (27-pound) beer keg over a bar set at 3.4 meters (11-feet).
E-10	In Mozambique, greetings are lengthy and involve inquiring into the health of each other's family. ▪ It's said that people from Bangladesh rarely smile because smiling is considered a sign of immaturity.
E-11	Daniel Tammet is an English autistic savant. He was able to recite Pi up to 22,514 digits. ▪ Shakuntala Devi (India) could make incredible calculations in her head. She was able to calculate the cube root of 61,629,875 in her head. (The answer is 395 x 395 x 395.)
E-12	In a book by Edgar Allan Poe, four survivors of a shipwreck decide to kill and eat the cabin boy, whose name was Richard Parker. Almost 150 years later, a boat sank with only four survivors, and the three senior members of the crew killed and ate the cabin boy, whose name was Richard Parker.

SET E

E-13	In Iceland, the telephone directory is listed alphabetically by first name rather than surname. ▪ In Portugal, the walls and floors of homes are decorated with tiles. ▪ In Jamaica, they drive on the left-hand side of the road.
E-14	Steffen Eliassen rode on a skateboard pulled by a car moving at 150 kilometres (93 miles) an hour. ▪ Sam Wakeling (UK) covered 170 kilometers (106 miles) on a unicycle without his feet even once touching the ground.
E-15	Bubble wrap was invented in 1957, but not on purpose. ▪ It was originally intended as a three-dimensional plastic wallpaper, but that proved to be commercially unsuccessful. ▪ Then, in 1961 it was sold as protective packaging.
E-16	In Japanese, there's a word to denote "a teenager who spends most of their time in their bedroom." ▪ In Hawaiian, there's a word for "scratching your head in order to remember something you have forgotten."
E-17	Ernest Loftus of Zimbabwe, Africa, kept a daily diary for over 91 years. He began his daily diary in 1896 at the age of 12 and continued it until his death in 1987 at the age of 103. ▪ A famous diary is that of Anne Frank (1929–1945) who wrote about life with her family hiding from the Nazis in World War Two.
E-18	There are now eco-friendly compostable straws. ▪ Researchers have developed a substance made from corn and soybeans which can be used to make edible plates and utensils. ▪ Scientists are working on creating edible packaging for cereal and pasta.

SET E

E-19	Over his lifetime, Barney Smith (1921–2019) designed, decorated, and collected roughly 1,400 toilet seat lids. ▪ Maurizio Savini (born in Brazil) uses chewed bubblegum to create sculptures. ▪ A painting created by an elephant named Ruby sold for $25,000.
E-20	When poet Amy Lowell (1874–1925) stayed in a hotel, she always rented the rooms above her, below her and on either side, in order to guarantee quiet. ▪ Actress Marlene Dietrich (1901–1992) liked to eat a sardine and onion sandwich as a cure for her insomnia.
E-21	Some of the strangest things that have been found at the London Transport Lost Property Office include: Two human skulls in a bag ▪ An urn filled with ashes ▪ Dead bats in a container ▪ A stuffed eagle ▪ A skeleton ▪ A box of false eyeballs.
E-22	When a boy fell through an enclosure at a zoo in 1996, a mother gorilla came to the rescue to protect him. She carried the injured boy around, guarding him against the other gorillas until zoo officials were able to safely remove the boy from the situation.
E-23	The universe is 13 billion years old. If the universe were just one year old, *Homo sapiens* (humans) would only have emerged at a few minutes before midnight on the last day of the year.
E-24	Sold on eBay: A man claimed he discovered the meaning of life and decided to sell it on eBay. His discovery sold for $3.26. ▪ Clippings of Justin Bieber's hair went for $40,668. ▪ A man auctioned the use of his forehead for advertising. He received $37,375 to advertise a snoring remedy.

SET E

E-25	A lizard smells through its forked tongue. ▪ An elephant can smell water up to 4.8 kilometers (3 miles) away. ▪ A male gorilla can eat 18 kilos (40 pounds) of food a day. ▪ Chimpanzees give a smile when they feel scared. ▪ A starving mouse will eat its own tail.
E-26	Human skin is completely replaced about 1,000 times during a person's life. ▪ James Allen, a 19th century outlaw, requested that when he died his skin be used to bind his autobiography to be presented to a former robbery victim.
E-27	A man in Connecticut (USA) divorced his wife because she left him a note on the refrigerator that read: "I won't be home when you return from work. I have gone to the bridge club. There will be a recipe for dinner at 7:00 o'clock on Channel 2."
E-28	In Costa Rica, grooms will publicly serenade their brides-to-be on the night before the wedding. ▪ At a wedding ceremony in the Indonesian Tidong tribe, the groom isn't allowed to see the bride's face until he sings her several love songs.
E-29	Ice cream was invented in China in A.D. 618 when King Tang employed 94 men to prepare his frozen goat's milk yogurt. ▪ Pizza originated in the year 100 B.C. in the Greek city of what is now Naples, Italy, when different toppings were added to flatbreads.
E-30	At age 17, soccer legend Pelé won the World Cup for Brazil and then passed out on the field. ▪ At age 18, Samantha Larson (USA) climbed the Seven Summits, the highest mountain on each of the seven continents.

SET E

E-31	Harry Houdini (1874–1926) was a Hungarian-born American magician and escape artist in the early 19th century. ▪ He could tie and untie knots in pieces of rope with his feet. ▪ He could undo the straps and buckles of a straitjacket with his teeth.
E-32	When Vera Czermak learned that her husband had been unfaithful, she decided to kill herself. So, she jumped out of her third-story window and landed on her husband who just happened to be passing by. She survived, but he died.
E-33	What do Cervantes, Hitler, and Marco Polo have in common? They all wrote books while they were in prison. ▪ What do France, Spain, the United States, China, and Italy have in common? In 2019, they were the countries that received the most tourists.
E-34	In their lifetime, the average human will: **(a)** spend a total of three years going to the bathroom; **(b)** produce 40,000 liters (10,500 gallons) of urine; **(c)** grow 950 kilometers (590 miles) of hair on their head; **(d)** talk for 12 years; and **(e)** blink 415 million times.
E-35	There's a species of cactus in Mexico that reaches nearly 21 meters (70 feet) in height. That's as tall as a 7-story building. ▪ There's a huge tree in California that has a hole in its trunk so that cars can drive through it.
E-36	Between 1725 and 1765, a peasant from Russia gave birth to 69 children, the greatest number of children born to one mother. In 27 pregnancies, she gave birth to 16 pairs of twins, 7 sets of triplets, and 4 sets of quadruplets.

SET E

E-37	In 1974, French high-wire artist Philippe Petit walked on a cable between the two Twin Towers of the New York World Trade Center, 110 floors above the ground. He has also walked between the towers of the Sydney Harbor Bridge in Australia.
E-38	If you're afraid of heights, you wouldn't want to walk on the Glass Footbridge in Hunan, China. This glass-bottomed bridge offers you a view of the valley 260 meters (853 feet) below. That's like looking out of the window on the 85th floor of a skyscraper.
E-39	French actress Sarah Bernhardt (1844–1923) kept a satin-lined coffin in her bedroom and occasionally slept in it. ▪ Rock musician Frank Zappa (1940-1993) named his son "Dweezil," and his daughter "Moon Unit."
E-40	Retail Therapy is going shopping for the sole purpose of making yourself feel better. ▪ Internet Addiction Disorder is a medical condition in which people are unable to control the amount of time they spend online.
E-41	A medium-size cumulus cloud weighs about the same as 80 elephants. ▪ The world's tallest tree is in Redwood National Park in the state of California. It rises to 115 meters (379 feet) feet above the ground. That's as high as a 37-story skyscraper.
E-42	The shortest woman ever was Pauline Musters (1876–1895), a Dutch woman who measured 61 centimeters (2 feet) at the time of her death. That's slightly shorter than a six-month-old child. Not quite as tall as a stack of five cans of soup.

SET E

E-43	Ethel Granger holds the record for the narrowest waist. In 1939, her waist had a circumference of only 33 centimeters (13 inches). She used a corset (a tight-fitting piece of clothing common in the past) to reduce her waist size in order to please her husband.
E-44	The founder of *match.com*, the first online dating site, lost his girlfriend to a man she met on *match.com*. ▪ In online dating sites, you're more likely to come across a teacher than someone from any other profession.
E-45	For about $1,500, the Vidstone company offers a tombstone with an embedded solar-powered video panel. When the panel cover is flipped open by graveside visitors, the device plays a short video featuring special moments of the deceased person's life.
E-46	In Hong Kong, snakes are the chief ingredient in both a popular broth and in a potent wine. ▪ The daily dietary requirement of phosphorus, calcium, and iron can be obtained by eating 20 caterpillars.
E-47	When T. M. Zink died in 1930, he left just $5 to his daughter and nothing to his wife. The rest of his money was for a "womanless" library. It would only carry books written by men, and no ladies would be allowed inside. The court ruled against this will.
E-48	The largest restaurant in the world is Damascus Gate in Damascus, Syria, with 6.014 seats. ▪ The restaurant employees a staff of 1,800 workers. ▪ It serves Arabian, Indian, Chinese, Syrian, Iranian, and Middle Eastern cuisines.

SET E

E-49	Matthew Hall, a 16th century farmer, was presumed dead and put in a coffin. As he was being carried to his final resting place, the pallbearers accidentally dropped his coffin onto the road, reviving him and startling everyone in the funeral procession.
E-50	George Meegan, a British adventurer, walked from the southern tip of South America (Tierra del Fuego) to the northernmost part of Alaska. Over a period of seven years, he walked 31,000 kilometers (19,000 miles), taking approximately 41 million steps.
E-51	At age 98, Nola Ochs (USA) received her master's degree in liberal arts. ▪ At age 93, the British humorist P. G. Wodehouse worked on his 97th novel, was knighted, and died. ▪ At age 69, Noah Webster released the 1st edition of his famous dictionary.
E-52	In 2018, Ananta Ram, a motivational speaker from Nepal, spoke nonstop for 90 hours. That's over three and a half days and nights of nonstop speaking. ▪ Pastor Zach Zehnder of Cross Church (USA) once preached a sermon that lasted 53 hours, more than two days.
E-53	The first successful gas-driven car was built in 1885 by Karl Benz (1844–1929). It had three wheels, weighed 254 kilos (560 pounds), and had a speed of 16 km/h (10 mph) ▪ In 2005, Juan Montoya (Colombia) set a Formula One speed record of 372 km/h (231 mph).
E-54	Although Hetty Green (1834–1916) was incredibly rich, with millions of dollars in the bank, she was also a great miser. In fact, she was so stingy that her son had to have his leg amputated because of the delays in finding a free medical clinic.

SET E

E-55	American poet Amy Lowell (1874–1925) created a scandal by smoking cigars in public. ▪ American author and poet Edgar Allan Poe (1809–1849) was expelled from West Point Military Academy in 1831 for "gross neglect of duty and disobedience of orders."
E-56	In 1969, former Beatle John Lennon (1940–1980) and his wife Yoko Ono held a week-long Bed-In for Peace in their honeymoon suite in the Amsterdam Hilton Hotel as a form of public protest against the Vietnam War. ▪ Lennon's most famous song is "Imagine."
E-57	In 1990, in India, two Hindu brides married the wrong man in a double wedding, due to the brides' heavy veils. Nevertheless, the marriages were declared final by village elders.
E-58	"Catfish" McCarthy took a shower that lasted 14 days ▪ French pop singer and songwriter Claude Antoine François (1939–1978) was electrocuted when he tried to fix a broken light bulb while standing in a bathtub.
E-59	The 10 most expensive cities in 2019 were: **1.** Singapore **2.** Paris **3.** Hong Kong **4.** Zurich **5.** Geneva **6.** Osaka **7.** Seoul **8.** Copenhagen **9.** New York **10.** Tel Aviv.
E-60	The first execution by the electric chair took place in New York in 1890. William Kemmler was executed for killing his girlfriend with a hatchet. ▪ In 2013, Rigoberto Hernandez was sentenced to 7,000 years in prison for having shot and killed three people outside of a nightclub in Dallas, Texas.

Set F

F-1	Crocodiles have brains no larger than a cigar. The muscles that close a crocodile's jaws exert a force equivalent to a truck falling off a cliff, but the muscles that open them are so weak that they can be kept shut by a few rolls of duct tape.
F-2	When Pluto was re-classified as a dwarf planet, Neptune became the most distant planet from the Sun. ▪ It takes light from the sun a little more than four hours to reach Neptune. ▪ Neptune takes 165 Earth years to complete its orbit around the sun.
F-3	The human body is composed of about 30 trillion cells. ▪ The average human body contains enough carbon to make 900 pencils, enough fat to make seven bars of soap, and enough water to fill a 50-liter (13-gallon) barrel.
F-4	The largest tumor ever recorded was an ovarian cyst weighing 149 kilos (328 pounds) removed from a woman in Texas in 1905. ▪ In 2001, doctors in Singapore spent 103 hours (four straight days) separating a pair of Siamese twins who were conjoined at the head.
F-5	After Eliza Donnithorne (1821–1886) of Sydney, Australia, was jilted at the altar by her fiancé, she stopped all the clocks in her house, remained a recluse, never again leaving her house, and wore her wedding gown for the next 30 years.
F-6	The Bedouins are nomadic Arabic-speaking peoples of the Middle Eastern deserts. A Bedouin wedding feast includes egg-filled fish placed inside a chicken, which in turn is put inside a whole sheep, which is then roasted inside a camel.

SET F

F-7	Funny tombstones: Here lies the body of Emily White. She signaled left and then turned right. ▪ Here lies the body of Samuel Proctor, who lived and died without a doctor. ▪ Here lies Fred who was alive and is dead. There's no more to be said.
F-8	Iced tea was invented at the 1904 St. Louis World's Fair by an Englishman named Richard Blechynden. It was so hot that day that his tea wasn't selling. He had the idea of pouring it over ice, and it was an instant success.
F-9	Alexander Zass (1888–1962) was a Russian strongman known as "Iron Samson." He could carry a horse on his shoulders, bend iron bars into a U-shape, break chains around his chest by expanding his chest, and pound a nail through a thick board using only the palm of his bare hand.
F-10	At age 21, college dropout Steve Jobs (1955–2011) co-founded the Apple Computer Company. ▪ At age 21, Thomas Edison (1847–1931) created his first invention, an electric vote recorder. ▪ At age 22, Samuel Colt (1814–1862) patented the Colt six-shooter revolver.
F-11	Domingo Joaquim (Angola) can stretch his mouth open so wide that he can fit a soda can sideways between his lips. ▪ Dean Sheldon (USA) stuffed 21 live scorpions in his mouth and held them there for ten seconds. When asked about the experience, he said, "It wasn't too bad."
F-12	How many times could you clap in one minute? Well, Eli Bishop (USA) clapped an incredible 1,103 times. ▪ Spanish opera singer Plácido Domingo once received a standing ovation that lasted one hour and 20 minutes.

SET F

F-13	Norway is home to the world's longest road tunnel. It has a length of 24 kilometers (15 miles). ▪ In the past, the Fijians were cannibals, but cannibalism stopped around 1844 when Christian missionaries came to the islands.
F-14	In 1965, Randy Gardner, a 17-year-old high school student, stayed awake for 11 days and 25 minutes. ▪ In 1979, an Austrian man survived for 18 days without water when the police forgot him in a jail cell. ▪ In 1992, James Scott survived 43 days without food when he got lost in the Himalayas.
F-15	Icelandic has a word that describes "the weather that is nice to see, but not to be in." ▪ In Tagalog (spoken in the Philippines) there's a word that means "the feeling of butterflies in your stomach that you typically feel when something romantic happens."
F-16	Colombian Luis Garavito, nicknamed "the Beast," was a serial killer with 138 proven and 300 suspected victims. ▪ Richard Phillips (USA) spent 45 years behind bars for a crime he didn't commit. He was 72 when he was released. (See YouTube video.)
F-17	The Ecoalf company makes clothing using discarded fishing nets, plastics bottles, worn-out tires, and even coffee grinds. ▪ The Aday company makes its Waste Nothing Jacket from 41 recycled water bottles. ▪ Batoko makes swimwear out of recycled plastic.
F-18	Common cures for insomnia include: Drinking a cup of chamomile tea. ▪ Drinking a mug of hot milk with honey and a few drops of brandy. ▪ Eating potatoes which are warm or at room temperature before going to bed. ▪ Listening to the sounds of ocean noises.

SET F

F-19	Barack Hussein Obama Junior was the first African–American president of the United States. ▪ His father was from Kenya. ▪ His name, Barack, means "one who is blessed" in Swahili. ▪ In high school he was known as "O'Bomber" because of his skill in basketball.
F-20	The sun is 4.5 billion years old. ▪ You could fit around 1.3 million earths inside the sun. ▪ The sun's core is so hot that a piece the size of a pinhead would produce enough heat to kill a person who was 160 kilometers (99 miles) away.
F-21	There's a hill in New Zealand whose indigenous name has 85 letters. The name means "The summit where Tamatea, the man with the big knees, the climber of mountains, the land-swallower who travelled about, played his nose flute to his loved one."
F-22	The smallest pygmies are the Mbutsi from the Democratic Republic of the Congo (formally Zaire) in Central Africa. Adults have an average height of 1.37 meters (4 feet 6 inches). That's about the same height as a 10-year-old boy.
F-23	Charlotte Guttenberg (USA) holds two world records. ▪ She's the woman who has the most tattoos. ▪ And she's the most-tattooed female senior citizen. At the age of 69, she had tattoos on 98.75% of her body.
F-24	The electric eel can deliver an electric shock of 600 volts, enough to knock a fully grown horse off its feet. ▪ The howler monkey is the loudest land animal. Its calls can be heard from a distance of over 5 kilometers (3 miles). ▪ A woodpecker can peck 20 times per second. ▪ Lobsters' bladders are in their heads.

SET F

F-25	In Bangkok, two cats were married in a $20,000 wedding ceremony that included matching gold rings. ▪ The wedding ceremony of Chinese superstar Angelababy cost $31 million. The wedding cake was a 3 meter- (10-foot) cake shaped like a carousel.
F-26	The record for the heaviest baby was for a boy born to Carmelina Fidele in Italy in 1955. The boy weighed 10 kilos (22 pounds). That's the same as the average weight of an 11-month-old baby. Or about the same as a watermelon.
F-27	A future bride from the Igbo tribe of Nigeria provides her prospective husband with a list of dowry gifts he is obliged to present to her family. Also, couples aren't supposed to set their wedding date until their older siblings have been married.
F-28	Upon hearing a nurse tell a visitor that he was feeling better, Norwegian playwright Henrik Ibsen uttered his last words: "On the contrary." ▪ The last words of the American actor Douglas Fairbanks (1883–1939) were: "I've never felt better."
F-29	Contortionist Sofie Dossi, a young American of Arab and Italian descent, once went into a crowded In-N-Out fast-food restaurant, ordered a burger, and proceeded to eat it with her feet. ▪ Kaif Khan, of India, ate 65 grapes in three minutes using his foot.
F-30	The hamburger, a ground-meat patty between two slices of bread, was possibly first sold in the United States in 1895 by a Danish immigrant named Louis Lassen. It got its name when a traveler from Hamburg, Germany, named it after the place where he lived.

SET F

F-31	Pastor Lars Clausen (USA) rode a unicycle from the West Coast to the East Coast and back to the West Coast of the United States, a distance of 14,700 kilometers (9,125 miles). ▪ Rob Thomson (New Zealand) rode a skateboard from Switzerland to China.
F-32	In 1975, a man riding a moped in Bermuda was accidentally struck and killed by a taxi. One year later, this man's brother was struck and killed by the very same taxi, driven by the very same driver, and even carrying the very same passenger.
F-33	Ben Underwood (1992–2009) was known as "the boy who sees with sound." He was able to detect objects by making clicking noises with his tongue. The returning eco from the objects would let him know where the objects were. He was able to play basketball, ride a bicycle, take karate classes, go skateboarding, and much more.
F-34	The Māori name for New Zealand means "Land of the Long White Cloud." ▪ Romania with its many medieval castles was the source of inspiration for the book *Dracula*. ▪ The national instrument of Bulgaria is the gaida, more commonly known as a bagpipe.
F-35	Botox was originally used as a treatment for crossed eyes, a condition in which each eye looks in a different direction. ▪ That a Botox treatment would also cause facial wrinkles to disappear was an unexpected discovery that resulted in cosmetic uses for Botox.
F-36	The Burj Khalifa in Dubai is the tallest building in the world. The 163-story building is 830 meters (2,700 feet) tall. That's twice as tall as the former Twin Towers of the World Trade Center in New York. It has 57 elevators and 24,348 windows that need cleaning.

SET F

F-37	Statues in ancient Rome were often made with detachable heads so that the heads could be replaced by more popular personalities if desired. ▪ There were about 6,000 statues of Joseph Stalin (1878–1953) throughout the Soviet Union at the time of his death.
F-38	In 1978, Mickey Mouse became the first cartoon character to have a star on Hollywood Boulevard. ▪ Horror film star Bela Lugosi was buried in his Dracula cape. ▪ British film star Charlie Chaplin once took part in a Charlie Chaplin look-alike contest — and lost.
F-39	In the state of Indiana (USA), during the 19th century, a folk remedy for a head cold consisted of inhaling the smell from a dirty sock nine times. ▪ In England, during the 18th century, snails were boiled in tea water as a remedy for chest congestion.
F-40	In spite of having suffered a stroke, French microbiologist Louis Pasteur (1822–1895) continued to work and in 1885 developed a vaccine for rabies. ▪ Five years after he suffered a stroke, German composer Handel (1685–1759) composed the *Messiah*.
F-41	A Doberman pinscher named Khan saved a 17-month-old toddler from a deadly snake attack. When the snake approached the child, Khan tried to nudge her away. When she didn't move, he picked her up by her diaper and gently tossed her a few feet behind him.
F-42	Warren Nord and Thor Andersen exchanged the same Christmas card every year from 1930–87, a total of 57 years. ▪ In December 1975, Werner Erhard (USA) sent 62,824 Christmas cards. ▪ An average Canadian household sends and receives 18 cards each holiday season.

SET F

F-43	The world's longest stairway goes up the side of Mt. Niesen in Switzerland. It's 3.4 kilometers (2 miles) long, with 11,647 steps. The record time to the top is 1 hour and 2 minutes, which is like climbing to the top of the Empire State Building more than 7 times.
F-44	Adam Woldemarim, a 42-year-old Ethiopian immigrant, found a case with $221.510 in cash that someone had left in the back seat of his taxi, which he then took to the company's office. An hour later, a man who had won the money at a cassino hugged him and gave him a reward of $2,000.
F-45	Yellowstone National Park (USA) sits on top of a super volcano that could potentially release enough ash to blanket the ground across the United States from coast to coast. ▪ The last cataclysmic eruption of this hidden volcano occurred 640,000 years ago.
F-46	The human nose can distinguish 10,000 different smells. ▪ You will need to hold your nose if you go to the planet Uranus. Its atmosphere smells like rotten eggs. ▪ It's impossible to hum while holding your nose.
F-47	Using a pair of reverse-looking mirrored glasses, Plennie Wingo (1895–1993) walked backwards across the United States from the West Coast to the East Coast, took a ship to Germany, and continued walking backwards through Europe to Istanbul, Turkey.
F-48	Evil knievel (1938–2007) was an American daredevil known for his spectacular motorcycle jumps. ▪ In 1974, he attempted to cross the Snake River Canyon in a rocket-propelled motorcycle (he failed but survived the crash). ▪ Over the years he broke 433 bones.

SET F

F-49	When Dr. Leila Denmark (USA) retired in May 2001, at the age of 103, she was the oldest practicing physician ever. ▪ At the age of 17, Balamurali Ambati (born in India) graduated from Mount Sinai School of Medicine, becoming the world's youngest doctor.
F-50	Kim Peek (1951–2009) was an American savant. ▪ He could read a book two pages at a time by reading each page with one eye while maintaining all of the information. ▪ He could tell anyone what day of the week they were born on and what happened that day.
F-51	On her 77th birthday, Anna Harahuess (USA) received birthday cards from three grandchildren. One card was posted in Boston, another from Hawaii, and the third from the state of Virginia. By chance, all three had sent the same identical card.
F-52	Ten cities often considered to be the most beautiful cities in the world: **1.** Paris **2.** Rome **3.** Amsterdam **4.** Venice **5.** Rio de Janeiro **6.** Prague **7.** Cape Town **8.** Istanbul **9.** Budapest **10.** Bruges, Belgium.
F-53	What do Beethoven, Emily Dickinson, Isaac Newton, and Mother Teresa have in common? They never married. ▪ What do Russia, Japan, China, and India have in common? They have all landed a space probe on the moon.
F-54	At the age of three, Kim Ung-yong (South Korea) could speak German, English, Japanese, and Korean. ▪ At the age of four, he was able to solve calculus problems. ▪ When he was eight years old, he was invited to work at NASA.

SET F

F-55	The edible ice cream cone was born of necessity. According to one story, when an ice cream seller at the 1904 World's Fair ran out of dishes, he shaped waffles into cones and served his ice cream in them.
F-56	Edmonds, a city in the state of Washington, is home to a basketball court with a floor made from recycled tennis shoes. ▪ There's a company in Sweden that makes briefcases, luggage, and furniture from recycled trash.
F-57	Before a battle, the English pirate known as Blackbeard (1680–1718) would dress in black clothes, fasten several pistols to his chest, and put burning fuses in his beard and hair, which covered him in a blanket of thick smoke. He looked like a devil from hell.
F-58	Prior to founding the Boy Scouts in 1910, Baden Powell (1857–1941) worked as a British spy disguising himself as a butterfly collector, incorporating plans of military installations into his drawings of butterfly wings.
F-59	American inventor Thomas Adams (1818–1905) tried and failed to turn the latex "chicle" into rubber for use in tires. Then, around 1870, after talking with a drugstore owner, Adams had the idea of marketing chicle as chewing gum, later known as "Chiclets."
F-60	The climate is tropical across the majority of Brazil. ▪ Baseball is the most popular sport in Cuba. ▪ There are no snakes in New Zealand. ▪ There are no mosquitoes in Iceland. ▪ Donkeys and camels were first domesticated in Ethiopia. ▪ Bulgaria is the homeland of yogurt. Bulgarians call theirs "sour milk" and they think it's what makes them live long lives.

Part Two
Facts Presented by Topics

1. Animal champions 70
2. Animal curiosities 73
3. The global table 76
4. Breakfast around the world 78
5. Exotic foods 80
6. Weather extremes 81
7. Natural wonders 82
8. Man-made landmarks 84
9. Environmental concerns 86
10. Sporting countries 88
11. Fun country facts 89
12. City curiosities 93
13. Cultural do's and don'ts 95
14. New Year's traditions 97
15. Birthdays around the world 99
16. Young achievers 103
17. Older achievers 105
18. Interesting people 107
19. Curious deaths 113
20. Death by stupidity 115
21. Funny tombstones 117
22. Bizarre laws 118
23. Strange lawsuits 120
24. Stupid thieves 122
25. Unusual books 124
26. Crazy song titles 125
27. Superstitions 126
28. Curious inventions 128
29. When was it invented? 129
30. Unsolved mysteries 131

Animal Champions

1.	Biggest animal	The biggest animal is the blue whale. A huge blue whale caught in 1947 was longer than two city buses and weighed as much as a Boeing 767-300 with 351 passengers ready for takeoff.
2.	Biggest land animal	The biggest animal on land is the African bush elephant. ▪ An adult weighs over six tons. That's as much as two pickup trucks. ▪ It's about 6 meters (19.7 feet) long. That's longer than a car.
3.	Tallest animal	The tallest animal is the giraffe. The average male giraffe is around 5.5 meters (18 feet) tall. That's taller than two professional basketball players, one standing on the other's shoulders.
4.	Fastest land animal	The fastest land animal is the cheetah, found in Africa, Iran, Turkey, and Afghanistan. It can accelerate from 0 to 96 kilometers (60 miles) per hour in three seconds and can maintain that speed for short distances.
5.	Slowest mammal	The slowest mammal is the three-toed sloth of South America. ▪ It moves at a speed of about 2 meters (6.5 feet) a minute. ▪ At that speed it would take about 25 minutes to cross a soccer field.
6.	Biggest fish	The biggest fish is the whale shark. ▪ The whale shark is 12 meters (40 feet) long. That's about the length of three medium-size cars. ▪ It weighs 15 tons. That's heavier than 2 elephants.

ANIMAL CHAMPIONS

7. Heaviest flying bird	The heaviest flying bird is the kori bustard, of Africa. It can weigh up to 18 kilos (40 pounds), about the same as a 20-liter (5-gallon) bottle of water.
8. Biggest nonflying bird	The largest nonflying bird is the ostrich. ▪ It's 2.4 meters (8 feet) tall. That's about the same height as the top of the front door to your house. ▪ It can weigh up to 150 kilos (330 pounds).
9. Biggest reptile	The biggest reptile is the saltwater crocodile. ▪ It's 5 meters (16 feet) long. That's about the length of two horses. ▪ It can weigh more than a ton. About the same as 4 Bengal tigers.
10. Biggest turtle	The biggest turtle is the leatherback sea turtle. It's 2.1 meters (7 feet) long from the tip of the beak to the tip of the tail. It weighs up to 680 kilos (1,500 pounds). That's as much as five medium-size refrigerators.
11. Heaviest snake	The heaviest snake is the anaconda, found in the tropical rainforests of South America. ▪ It can have a circumference as big as a dinner plate. ▪ A huge anaconda killed in Brazil in 1960 weighed an estimated 227 kilos (500 pounds).
12. Longest snake	The longest snake is the reticulated python, found in Southeast Asian jungles. It can reach a length of 9 meters (29 feet). That's longer than 2 medium-size cars.

ANIMAL CHAMPIONS

13. Biggest frog	The biggest frog is the goliath frog of western Africa. Adults usually grow to around 30 centimeters (11.8 inches). That's longer than three mice. They can weigh as much as a newborn baby.
14. Biggest bat	The biggest bat is the flying fox, found in the Philippines. ▪ Flying fox bats have a wingspan of 1.7 meters (5 feet 7 inches). That's almost as long as a twin-size bed. ▪ They can weigh more than a large pineapple.
15. Heaviest insect	The heaviest insect is the giant weta, found off the New Zealand coast. It can weigh as much as two mice.
16. Biggest spider	The biggest spider is the goliath bird-eating spider, found in the rainforests of South America. ▪ With its legs extended it can be the size of a large dinner plate. ▪ It weighs as much as a medium-size apple.

Animal Curiosities

1. Alligator	An adult human could hold the jaws of an alligator shut with their bare hands.
2. Bat	A single bat can eat more than 600 bugs in one hour, which is like a person eating 20 pizzas for dinner. A small colony of bats can eat over one ton of insects in one year, or more than 600 million bugs.
3. Bear	A full-grown bear can run as fast as a horse.
4. Camel	A camel can survive up to six months without food or water.
5. Cat	There are over 500 million domestic cats in the world.
6. Cheetah	Cheetahs cannot climb trees and have poor night vision.
7. Dog	A dog's sense of smell is 10,000 and perhaps up to 100,000 times better than a human's.
8. Eagle	Eagles have excellent eyesight. They can spot a rabbit from a distance of 3.3 kilometers (2 miles).
9. Elephant	Elephant teeth can weigh as much as 4 kilos (9 pounds).
10. Frog	Frogs can see forwards, sideways and upwards, all at the same time. They never close their eyes, even when they sleep.

ANIMAL CURIOSITIES

11.	Giant panda	The giant panda, or simply the panda, is native to China. At birth, a panda is smaller than a mouse.
12.	Giraffe	A giraffe has the same number of bones in its neck as a human, which is also the same number for a mouse (seven bones).
13.	Gorilla	Gorillas are highly intelligent. In fact, Koko, a gorilla born in a zoo, was taught to use sign language and had an active vocabulary of more than 1,000 signs.
14.	Green anaconda	The green anaconda squeezes its prey to death and then swallows it whole. The special structure of its jaws permits it to swallow animals as large as wild pigs, deer, or alligators.
15.	Hippo	The name hippopotamus means "river horse" and is often shortened to "hippo." They can run faster than humans.
16.	Horse	Horses have the biggest eyes of the mammals that live on land.
17.	Kangaroo	At birth baby kangaroos are only about 2.5 centimeters (one inch) in length. That's smaller than two grapes.
18.	Leopard	Leopards protect their food from other animals by dragging it high up in a tree.
19.	Lion	The roar of a lion can be heard from 8 kilometers (5 miles) away.

ANIMAL CURIOSITIES

20.	Octopus	A female octopus lays on average about 200,000 eggs; however, only a handful will hatch and survive.
21.	Ostrich	Ostriches can run faster than horses, and the males can roar like lions.
22.	Owl	Most owls are nocturnal, so they sleep during the day and hunt at night. Their ears that are so good that they can hear a mouse move two feet under the surface of the snow.
23.	Penguin	Penguins are flightless birds. ▪ Most penguins live in the Southern Hemisphere. ▪ None live in Alaska or at the North Pole.
24.	Pig	Pigs are among the most intelligent animals in the world, along with chimpanzees, dolphins, elephants, and even octopuses. There are around 2 billion pigs in the world.
25.	Polar bear	Polar bears have an excellent sense of smell. They can detect seals nearly 1.6 kilometers (one mile) away.
26.	Rhinoceros	The name rhinoceros means "nose horn" and is often shortened to "rhino."
27.	Seal	Some seals can stay underwater for up to an hour without taking a breath.
28.	Skunk	A skunk's spray is powerful enough to drive away a bear. The smell can be detected by a human 1,600 meters (one mile) away.

The Global Table

1.	Brazil	A popular dish in Brazil is *feijoada*, a thick stew made with black beans, beef tongue, pork, and smoked sausages. It's served with rice, farofa (toasted cassava) and stir-fried collard greens.
2.	Costa Rica	A popular dish in Costa Rica is *gallo pinto*. It's made with beans and rice cooked together with a traditional sauce.
3.	Cuba	A popular dish in Cuba is *picadillo*, a mixture of ham, beef, raisins, olives, potatoes, with rice and fried eggs.
4.	Ethiopia	A popular dish in Ethiopia is *wat*, a thick chicken, beef or lamb stew with a variety of vegetables. This is eaten by scooping it up with *injera*, a gray and slightly spongy flat bread.
5.	France	A popular dish in France is the crêpe, a very thin pancake with a filling. Sweet fillings include chocolate sauce, jelly, and preserves. Savory (salty) fillings include ham, sausage, cheese, and mushrooms.
6.	Greece	A popular dish in Greece is *moussaka*, a casserole made with eggplant, spicy ground lamb, and topped with a thick white sauce.
7.	Hungary	A popular dish in Hungary is *Hungarian goulash*, a spicy stew of meat, noodles, and potatoes, seasoned with paprika.

THE GLOBAL TABLE

8. India	A popular dish in India is *tandoori* chicken, a chicken marinated in yoghurt and spices, and baked in a traditional Indian clay oven.
9. Ireland	A popular dish in Ireland is Irish stew, a stew made with mutton, potatoes, onions, carrots, and parsley.
10. Korea	A popular dish in Korea is *kimchi*, a spicy side dish made with pickled cabbage and other vegetables.
11. Morocco	A popular dish in Morocco is *tagine*, a lamb, goat or chicken stew with spices, nuts, olives, and citrus fruits.
12. Peru	A popular dish in Peru is *ceviche*, raw fish and seafood marinated in lime or lemon juice.
13. Romania	A popular dish in Romania consists of sweet peppers stuffed with ground pork or beef, herbs and rice, baked in a tomato sauce.
14. Russia	A popular dish in Russia is *borscht*, a beet soup that is served hot or cold, often with a big dollop of sour cream and a plate of savory pastries called *piroshki*.
15. Scotland	A popular dish in Scotland is *haggis*. This is made from the heart, liver and lungs of a sheep, which are cut up, blended with oatmeal, and boiled in the stomach of the animal.

Breakfast around the World

1.	Argentina	A common breakfast in Argentina is a cup of strong coffee or steamed milk with bittersweet chocolate melted into it. This is often accompanied by sweet rolls.
2.	Australia	A hearty breakfast in Australia will frequently include bacon, eggs, sausages, grilled tomato and mushrooms, and hash browns or beans.
3.	Canada	Traditional breakfast foods in Canada are eggs, fried pork, bacon or sausages, fried or deep-fried potatoes, toast, and pancakes with maple syrup.
4.	Colombia	Breakfast in Colombia often includes a soup made with milk, water, and potatoes, typically served with an egg on top. This is served with stale bread used to soak up the creamy broth.
5.	Denmark	On the breakfast table in Denmark you will often find rye bread, rolls, cheeses, salami, ham, pâté, honey, jam, and Danish pastries.
6.	Dominican Republic	The breakfast table in the Dominican Republic has tropical fruits, such as bananas, passion fruit, papaya, mangoes, pineapples, as well a traditional dish of mashed boiled plantains.
7.	England	A full English breakfast has eggs, bacon, sausages, baked beans, grilled tomato, crumpets, toast, and hash browns.

BREAKFAST AROUND THE WORLD

8. Germany	Breakfast in Germany consists of German sausages, local cheeses, cold cuts, freshly baked bread, jams and honey for the bread, and perhaps an egg or two.
9. Ghana	One of the most popular breakfast dishes in Ghana is rice cooked in beans. This is often topped with fish, egg, spaghetti, fried plantain, and avocado.
10. Holland	In Holland, a typical breakfast might have cheese, cold cuts, and toast topped with jam, honey, apple syrup, a chocolate spread, or *hagelslag* (sweet chocolate sprinkles).
11. Japan	Breakfast in Japan is white rice, accompanied by small dishes of miso soup, tofu, grilled fish, Japanese pickles, and edible seaweed.
12. Jordan	On the breakfast table in Jordan you will find mortadella, lamb sausage, yogurt cheese, hummus, falafel, pita bread, olives, dates, jam and butter.
13. Malaysia	A popular breakfast in Malaysia is rice cooked in coconut milk. This is often served with peanuts, sliced cucumber, boiled eggs, deep-fried anchovies, and a hot sauce.
14. Pakistan	A breakfast in Pakistan might be eggs, flat bread stuffed with spicy mashed potatoes, a yogurt-based drink, fruits, honey, and small patties of minced meat.
15. Poland	A breakfast in Poland might consist of scrambled eggs with slices of Polish sausage, joined by two potato pancakes. (a fried pancake made with grated potatoes).

Exotic Foods

1.	Ant eggs	In the Philippines, they eat ant eggs. The eggs are fried in butter, leaving the outsides crispy and the insides creamy.
2.	Bats	Bat paste is a delicacy in Thailand. A live bat is put in boiling milk. Once it becomes soft, it's mashed and made into a paste.
3.	Chicken feet	Chicken feet are eaten in East Asia, the Caribbean, South Africa, and South America. First, they are simmered and seasoned.
4.	Cockroaches	In Thailand, large cockroaches are roasted and then eaten. Roasted beetles are also popular.
5.	Dogs	Dog meat is a popular food item in the Philippines, China, Korea, Vietnam, and various other countries.
6.	Monkey brains	In China, monkey brains are considered a delicacy. The brain is eaten raw, fried, or cooked with a variety of spices.
7.	Snails	In France, snails are cooked in a sauce of white wine, garlic and butter, and served in their shells.
8.	Tarantulas	In Cambodia, giant tarantulas are deep fried and seasoned with garlic and salt.
9.	Tuna eyeballs	In Japan, the giant eyeballs of the tuna fish are boiled or sautéed. They're often served with a slice of lemon and soy sauce.

Weather Extremes

1.	Hottest place	In Dallol, Ethiopia, the average temperature is 34° C (94° F).
2.	Hottest recorded temperature	The hottest recorded temperature on the planet was 58° C (136.4° F). That was in Libya in 1922.
3.	Coldest average temperature	At Plateau Station in Antarctica, the average temperature is minus 58° C (minus 72° F).
4.	Coldest recorded temperature	The coldest recorded temperature was in Antarctica in 1983. The temperature was minus 89° C (minus 128° F).
5.	Most rainy days	Mount Waialeale, a volcano in Hawaii, is one of the rainiest spots on the planet. It rains up to 350 days a year.
6.	Windiest place	The windiest place on the planet is in Antarctica. Winds of 241 kilometers (150 miles) per hour are common.
7.	Greatest recorded snowfall	The greatest recorded snowfall was in Colorado (USA) in 1921. Within 24 hours, almost 2 meters (6 feet) of snow fell. Taller than the average man.
8.	Largest hailstone	The largest hailstone fell in South Dakota (USA) in 2010. It was nearly as big as a volleyball and weighed 0.87 kilos, almost two pounds.

Natural Wonders

1.	Amazon rainforest	The Amazon rainforest is the world's largest tropical rainforest. Some common animals that live in the rainforest are jaguars, monkeys, sloths, anacondas, alligators, piranhas, poisonous frogs, and venomous snakes.
2.	Angel Falls	Angel Falls, in the jungles of Venezuela, is the highest waterfall in the world. ▪ It has a total drop of 979 meters (3,212 feet). ▪ A skyscraper that tall would have 320 stories.
3.	Aurora borealis	The aurora borealis is a luminous display of lights in the sky seen in the artic regions of Alaska, northern Canada, and Greenland. They often resemble red, yellow, green, blue, or violet dancing curtains. It's also called the northern lights.
4.	Grand Canyon	The Grand Canyon is a spectacular canyon in Arizona (USA). ▪ It's 446 kilometers (277 miles) long. ▪ Parts of the canyon are 1.6 kilometers (1 mile) deep and 29 kilometers (18 miles) wide.
5.	Harbor of Rio de Janeiro	The Harbor of Rio de Janeiro is strikingly beautiful. On a peninsula in the bay is the famous Sugarloaf Mountain, 396 meters (1,299 feet) high, known for its cableway and panoramic views of the city and beyond.

NATURAL WONDERS

6. Mount Everest	Mount Everest is the highest mountain in the world. It's in Nepal and Tibet. ▪ It's 8,932 meters (29,305 feet) high. ▪ The first mountaineers to reach the summit were Edmund Hillary and Tenzing Norgay in 1953.
7. Old Faithful	Old Faithful is a geyser in Yellowstone National Park. ▪ Its eruption reaches a height of 44 meters (145 feet), as high as a 14-story building. ▪ The eruptions occur every 90 minutes.
8. Paricutin volcano	Paricutin is the youngest volcano in the Western Hemisphere. ▪ It began in a corn field in Mexico in 1943. ▪ Within two months the cone of the volcano was 300 meters (1,000 feet) high. ▪ The last eruption was in 1952.
9. Sahara Desert	The Sahara Desert in North Africa is the largest hot desert in the world. ▪ It's about the same size as the United States. ▪ Some of its sand dunes are 150 meters (500 feet) high, taller than a 40-story building.
10. Victoria Falls	Victoria Falls in Africa is often called the largest waterfall in the world. ▪ The falling water causes a thunderous noise and a cloud of vapor which can be seen and heard miles away. ▪ It was named after England's Queen Victoria.

Man-Made Landmarks

1.	Australia	A famous landmark in Australia is the Opera House in Sidney, a huge building shaped like the sails of a boat. There are over one million tiles on its roof.
2.	Brazil	A famous landmark in Brazil is the Statue of Christ the Redeemer. ▪ The statue sits on the peak of a mountain overlooking the city of Rio de Janeiro. ▪ The statue is 30 meters (98 feet) tall. ▪ The iconic outstretched arms are 28 meters (92 feet) wide.
3.	China	A famous landmark in China is the Great Wall. ▪ This wall is actually a series of walls 22,000 kilometers (13,670 miles) long. ▪ The walls were built over a period of 2,000 years ending around the 17th century.
4.	Egypt	A famous landmark in Egypt is the Great Sphinx, a huge stone sculpture of a mythical creature with a human head and a lion's body. ▪ Its body is 60 meters (200 feet) long and 20 meters (65 feet) tall. ▪ It was built around 4,500 years ago.
5.	England	A famous landmark in England is the Clock Tower, known as Big Ben. ▪ It's 96 meters (315 feet) tall, as tall as a 30-story building. ▪ The clock took 13 years to build and began ticking in 1858.
6.	France	A famous landmark in France is the Eiffel Tower, designed by Gustave Eiffel to be the main attraction for the 1889 World Fair in Paris. It's 300 meters (980 ft) tall and covered with 20,000 sparkling lights.

MAN-MADE LANDMARKS

7.	India	A famous landmark in India is Taj Mahal, a white marble mausoleum built in the 17th century by an emperor in memory of his wife who died in childbirth. In the morning it appears pink; in the afternoon, bright white; in the moonlight, golden.
8.	Italy	A famous landmark in Italy is the Leaning Tower of Pisa, a bell tower that isn't vertical. ▪ When the second story was built in 1178, the tower began to lean. ▪ It was finally completed 200 years later in 1372. ▪ There are 297 steps to the top of the tower.
9.	Mexico	A famous landmark in Mexico is the Pyramid of the Sun. Although it was given this name by the Aztecs, it was actually built by a previous civilization. It's 66 meters (720 feet) high. There are 248 uneven steps up to the top.
10.	Peru	A famous landmark in Peru is Machu Picchu, an ancient city built by the Incas high up in the Andes Mountains. ▪ There were houses, agricultural terraces, temples, and even an observatory to look at the stars. ▪ It was built around 1450 but abandoned in 1572.
11.	Russia	A famous landmark in Russia is Saint Basil's Cathedral, located in the area called the Red Square. ▪ The 32-meter (107-foot-) tall cathedral is surrounded by eight tower-like chapels with distinctive onion-shaped domes. ▪ It was commissioned by the Czar known as Ivan the Terrible.

Environmental Concerns

1. The Amazon rainforest is often called the lungs of the planet. ▪ It releases a significant amount of oxygen into the air. ▪ It removes carbon dioxide from the air, which reduces global warming by lowering the planet's greenhouse gas levels.

2. Logging has reduced the size of the Amazon rainforest by 20% in just 40 years. ▪ Every year 52,000 square kilometers (20,000 square miles) disappear. That's an area about the size of Costa Rica.

3. Every day 27,000 trees are cut down so we can have toilet paper. ▪ It takes about 75,000 trees to produce the Sunday edition of the *New York Times*.

4. If the current rate of destruction continues, by the year 2100 the world's rainforests will be gone or almost completely gone.

5. Paper can only be recycled six times. After that, the fibers are too weak to hold together.

6. Recycling one aluminum can saves enough energy to run a TV for three hours. ▪ About 80 trillion aluminum cans are used by humans every year.

7. The United States is the No. 1 trash-producing country in the world. If the entire world lived like the average American, we would need five planets to provide enough resources.

8. The average American home uses over 379,000 liters (100,000 gallons) of water every year. ▪ It takes more than 15,000 liters (4,000 gallons) of water to produce 1 kilo (2 pounds) of beef. ▪ By the year 2040, the planet will experience severe water shortages.

ENVIRONMENTAL CONCERNS

9. If current patterns continue, by the year 2050 we will have emptied the oceans of seafood. ▪ By the year 2070, the world's coral reefs could be gone altogether.

10. Climate change is causing the polar ice caps to melt, which in turn is threatening the existence of polar bears.

11. By the end of the century, half of the species of animals could be facing extinction. ▪ The current list of endangered species includes the black rhino, orangutan, Asian elephant, blue whale, chimpanzee, and the mountain gorilla.

12. About 35% of a landfill is packaging materials.

13. Here is the time it takes for some things to decompose: cotton (about 5 months)   leather shoe (40 years)   tin can (50 years)   aluminum can (200 years)   plastic bottle (450 years)   plastic bag (1,000 years)   glass bottle (never really decomposes)

14. We use an incredible five trillion plastic bags per year.

15. The equivalent of one garbage truck of plastic is dumped into our oceans every single minute. ▪ By 2030, it will be two truckloads per minute, and by 2050, four.

16. By 2050, measured by weight, there could be more plastic than fish in the world's oceans.

17. The world population is growing by about 80 million people every year. ▪ By the year 2100, we will produce three times more waste than we do today.

Sporting Countries

Sport	Where it originated
1. Beach soccer	Brazil
2. Bowling	Germany
3. Boxing	Italy (ancient Rome)
4. Bull fighting	Spain
5. Chess	India
6. Golf	Scotland
7. Gymnastics	Greece
8. Ice hockey	Canada
9. Ice skating	Netherlands
10. Judo	Japan
11. Ping-Pong	England
12. Skiing	Norway
13. Soccer	England
14. Surfing	Polynesia
15. Tennis	France
16. Volleyball	United States

Fun Country Facts

1.	Argentina	Argentina is known for the *tango*, a graceful, provocative, melancholic, romantic dance with synchronized movements.
2.	Australia	Australia was originally settled by the British as a prison colony. Starting in 1788, convicts from England, Ireland, Scotland, and Wales were sent to Australia.
3.	Belgium	Belgium is world-famous for its chocolate, waffles, and beer. There are over 1,100 varieties of beers made in Belgium.
4.	Bolivia	There are 37 official languages in Bolivia—Spanish and 36 indigenous languages. Indigenous people make up about two-thirds of its population.
5.	Brazil	Brazil is famous for its world-cup-winning national soccer teams; soccer superstar Pelé; carnival in Rio de Janeiro; a dance called the *samba*; a type of music called *bossa nova*; and its soap operas.
6.	Bulgaria	Bulgarians shake their head when they mean to say "yes" and nod when they want to say "no."
7.	Cambodia	The present (2020) king of Cambodia, King Sihamoni, is a trained ballet dancer. He graduated in classical music and dance, and taught dance in Paris, where he had his own ballet group.

FUN COUNTRY FACTS

8. Chile	One of the oldest mummies in the world was discovered in Chile. It's from 5050 B.C., which is 2,000 years older than the Egyptian mummies.
9. Colombia	In Colombia, it's mandatory for radio and television to play the national anthem every day at 6 a.m. and 6 p.m.
10. Cuba	From the air, Cuba resembles a crocodile or an alligator. Its handcrafted cigars are considered the finest cigars in the world.
11. Denmark	Denmark has a place to surf called Cold Hawaii, and it's one of the best beaches in Scandinavia for surfing.
12. Ethiopia	Some of the earliest ancestors of modern humans lived in Ethiopia over two million years ago.
13. Finland	In Finland, there's a sport called "wife carrying." The first prize is your wife's weight in beer.
14. Ghana	Traditionally in Ghana, a widow is expected to be married to a living brother of her deceased husband.
15. Guatemala	Guatemala, home to the ancient Mayans, was possibly the birthplace of chocolate. One more fact: the national instrument of Guatemala is the marimba.
16. Iceland	Despite its name, Iceland is not covered in ice, and it has surprisingly mild winters. Icelanders joke that they should be Greenland, and Greenland should be Iceland.

FUN COUNTRY FACTS

17. India	India has a spa just for elephants. The elephants receive baths, massages, and even food.
18. Indonesia	Indonesia is home to the world's largest flower (*Rafflesia arnoldii*), which may also be the world's stinkiest.
19. Iran	Iran used to be known as Persia. Iran gave us Persian rugs, the Persian cat, and indirectly the word "paradise" which originally meant an "enclosed garden."
20. Jamaica	Jamaica is home to reggae music, musician Bob Marley, and Olympic runner Usain Bolt, the fastest man in the world.
21. Jordan	In Jordan, if you don't want more coffee, you need to shake the hand holding the cup from side to side. Otherwise, your cup will be refilled.
22. Kenya	Kenya has many wildlife reserves that offer safaris where large animals, such as lions, elephants, buffalos, leopards, and rhinoceros can be seen in their natural habitat.
23. Mexico	Bullfighting is a 500-year-old traditional sport in Mexico that takes place in a stadium called a "bullring."
24. Morocco	White is the color of mourning in Morocco. A Moroccan widow wears white for 40 days after the death of her husband.

FUN COUNTRY FACTS

25.	Netherlands	The Netherlands is also known as Holland. There are still over 1,000 working traditional windmills in the Netherlands.
26.	New Zealand	In 1893, New Zealand became the first country in the world to give women the right to vote.
27.	Nigeria	Nigeria's movie industry is known as "Nollywood." It is one of the largest movie industries in the world.
28.	Panama	Panama is the only place in the world where you can see the sun rise in the Pacific and set in the Atlantic.
29.	Portugal	The Portuguese introduced tea drinking to England and *tempura* cooking to Japan.
30.	Romania	Romania is home to the "Merry Cemetery." Each gravestone is carved in bright, cheerful colors and contains a poem, often with a humorous message from the person buried there.
31.	Sweden	The Swedish passport is among the best in the world. Someone with a Swedish passport can enter 124 countries without a visa.
32.	Switzerland	The Swiss eat more chocolate than any other nation in the world, an average of 11 kilos (24 pounds) per year.
33.	Tanzania	Tanzania is home to the world's only tree climbing lions and Tingatinga paintings, a painting style that uses bold vibrant colors and simple African images.

City Curiosities

1. Amsterdam, Netherlands	Amsterdam has more bikes than people. There are approximately 870,000 inhabitants and one million bikes.
2. Berlin, Germany	Berlin was the first city in Europe to have traffic lights.
3. Bogotá, Colombia	The streets in Bogotá don't have names. They have numbers.
4. Brasília, Brazil	Brasília, the capital of Brazil, looks like an airplane when viewed from above. It was officially inaugurated in 1960.
5. Budapest	Budapest consists of two parts, Buda and Pest, which are situated on opposite sides of the Danube River.
6. Buenos Aires	Dinner is served very late in Buenos Aires, usually after 9 p.m.
7. Chicago, USA	The zipper, the vacuum cleaner, spray-paint and the Ferris wheel were all born in Chicago.
8. Damascus, Syria	Damascus is the oldest existing city. It has been inhabited for over 11,000 years.
9. Dublin, Ireland	Dublin was founded by the Vikings in the 9th century. It has a pub that was established over 850 years ago.

CITY CURIOSITIES

10. Hong Kong, China	Hong Kong has the largest number of Rolls-Royce cars per resident in the entire world.
11. Lhasa, Tibet	Lhasa, Tibet, is the highest capital city in the world. It's 3,636 meters (12,087 feet) above sea level.
12. Luanda, Angola	The official language of Luanda, Angola, is Portuguese.
13. Madrid, Spain	Madrid had its origin in the 9th century, when the Moors built forts and a wall around the city.
14. Manila, Philippines	Binondo, a district in Manila, is the oldest Chinatown in the world. It was established in 1594.
15. Monte Carlo, Monaco	Monte Carlo is the only city with an orchestra that's larger than the country's army.
16. New York City	The first pizzeria in the United States opened in New York City in 1895.
17. Paris, France	There are no stop signs in Paris.
18. Quito, Ecuador	Quito was the first city to be declared a UNESCO World Heritage Site.
19. Reykjavik, Iceland	Reykjavik is the northernmost capital city in the world. During the summer, the sun shines for 21 hours each day.
20. Tokyo, Japan	Tokyo really glows. It has more neon signs than any other city in the world.

Cultural Do's and Don'ts

1. Afghanistan	In Afghanistan and throughout the Muslim world, eat your food with your right hand, not your left.
2. Brazil	In Brazil, don't ask if the capital is Buenos Aires. ▪ The capital is Brasília, an ultramodern city in the middle of the country. ▪ Brazil and Argentina are neighbors and rivals.
3. Canada	In Canada, not holding a door open for another person is considered impolite.
4. China	In China, if you clean your plate, the host will be offended because it's a sign that you didn't get enough food.
5. Denmark	If you're invited to a Danish home, be punctual.
6. England	In England, cutting in line, known as "jumping the queue," is seriously frowned upon.
7. France	Don't bring wine as a gift in France. It's an insult that suggests that the host could not provide the guests with good wine.
8. Germany	In Germany, use utensils, not your fingers, to eat—even foods like pizza and fries. The one exception is bread.
9. India	In India, hugging and handshakes are still frowned upon in most parts of the country among members of opposite sex.

CULTURAL DO'S AND DON'TS

10. Japan	Always take off your shoes before going into a Japanese home.
11. Kenya	In Kenya, finish everything on your plate, or the host will be offended and think you didn't like the food.
12. Korea	In Korea, you should be quiet on public transportation. Noisiness is considered very rude.
13. Kuwait	In Kuwait, when the host stands, the meal is over.
14. Mexico	In Mexico, it's considered rude to ask how much a person earns.
15. Middle East	If you are a man, don't go giving handshakes to women in the Middle East.
16. Pakistan	In Pakistan, arrive about 15 minutes after the scheduled time of a meal and up to one hour after the start of a party.
17. Scandinavia	In Scandinavia, don't forget to say "Thank you for the meal." It's a MUST.
18. Singapore	In Singapore, you can get fined for feeding the birds, spitting, smoking in public, eating or drinking on public transportation, and littering.
19. USA	In the United States, don't forget to leave a tip after your meal at a restaurant. Taxi drivers, hairdressers, hotel workers, and many others also expect to be tipped.

New Year's Traditions

1.	Australia	In Australia, the new year is brought in with midnight displays of fireworks, one of the most important being from the Sydney Harbor Bridge, which draws huge crowds.
2.	Brazil	In Brazil, on New Year's Eve, people wear white to bring peace, harmony, and happiness, as well as to chase away evil spirits. ▪ Other Brazilian traditions include throwing white flowers into the sea and jumping over seven waves. You get one wish for each wave.
3.	Chile	In Chile, on New Year's Eve, families go to the cemetery to ring in the new year with their deceased relatives, much like Mexico's Day of the Dead.
4.	Colombia	New Year's Eve traditions in Colombia include having cash in the pocket for good financial luck and taking the first step after midnight with the right foot for a positive start in the new year.
5.	Ecuador	In Ecuador, New Year's Eve festivities include bonfires burning large puppets of politicians and other disliked people.
6.	Greece	The Greeks ring in the new year by eating a sweet bread called St. Basil's cake, which has a coin baked inside. Whoever gets the slice with the coin will have good luck for the next year.

NEW YEAR'S TRADITIONS

7. Ireland	The Irish have a tradition of banging bread against the walls of their house on New Year's Eve. Bad luck and evil spirits are chased away, and good luck is invited in.
8. Japan	In Japan, on New Year's Eve, Buddhist temples ring their bells 108 times to expel the 108 types of human weakness. Houses are cleaned, and misunderstandings are supposed to be forgiven.
9. Puerto Rico	New Year's Eve traditions in Puerto Rico include dumping a bucket of water out the window to drive away evil spirits and sprinkling sugar outside their houses to invite good luck in.
10. Russia	In Russia, on New Year's Eve, people write down their wishes for the coming year, burn the paper they wrote it on, and drink the ashes in a glass of champagne.
11. Spain	In Spain, on New Year's Eve, people eat twelve green grapes at midnight, one for each month of the new year. The tradition is meant to secure twelve happy months in the coming year.
12. USA	New Year's Eve traditions in the United States include parties, fireworks displays, kissing at midnight, singing "Auld Lang Syne" ("for the sake of old times") and making of New Year's resolutions, such as to go on a diet, to exercise more, to be more organized, etc.

Birthdays around the World

1.	Argentina	In Argentina, the birthday child receives a pull on the earlobe for each year they have been alive.
2.	Australia	At birthday parties in Australia, children eat "fairy bread" buttered bread covered with candy sprinkles and typically cut into triangles.
3.	Brazil	In Brazil, the birthday celebration is often a big party in a rented hall. There's always an elaborate table filled with sweets, especially fudge balls, and children leave with a party gift bag.
4.	Canada	In Canada, birthday cakes for children are decorated with colored sprinkles with a wrapped coin hidden inside. Whoever finds the coin, gets the first turn in all the party games.
5.	Denmark	In Denmark, a flag is flown outside a window to designate that someone living in that house is having a birthday.
6.	Ecuador	In Ecuador, when a girl turns 15, there's a big celebration, and the girl wears a pink dress. The father dances a waltz with her, while 14 other girls and 14 other boys also dance the waltz.
7.	Egypt	In Egypt, birthday parties are full of singing and dancing. Egyptians usually have a birthday cake, but they don't send one another birthday cards.

BIRTHDAYS AROUND THE WORLD

8. England	In England, it's traditional for the birthday child to have "the bumps." Friends lift the child up and down, bumping them gently on the ground, one bump for each year, and one for good luck.
9. Germany	In Germany, parents like to wake up the birthday child with a cake and birthday candles. The candles stay lit until after dinner, when everyone sings the birthday song.
10. Ghana	In Ghana, the birthday child gets a special breakfast treat of deep-fried sweet-potato patties. Later in the day, there may be a party where they eat stew, rice, and fried plantains.
11. Hungary	In Hungary, it's traditional to pull the ear of the birthday person, while reciting a poem wishing them a life as long as their ears will be when they touch the floor.
12. India	In India, on the day of their birthday, children wear very colorful clothing to school and pass out chocolates to the entire class. They also kneel and touch their parents' feet as a sign of respect.
13. Ireland	In Ireland, on their birthday, an adult will hear Irish toasts and blessings, such as "May you live to be a hundred years and an extra year to repent." and "May you be an hour in heaven before the devil knows you are dead."

BIRTHDAYS AROUND THE WORLD

14. Israel	In Israel, the birthday child sits in a chair decorated with streamers. ▪ Guests sing and dance around the chair, raising and lowering the chair, once for each year of age, plus one more time for good luck.
15. Jamaica	In Jamaica, it's traditional for the birthday boy or girl to be covered in flour. This often happens at a party with dancing to reggae music.
16. Malaysia	In Malaysia, friends or relatives give the person celebrating their birthday a present or a small red packet filled with money.
17. Mexico	In a child's birthday party in Mexico, a piñata (a paper-mache object filled with candy) is hung from the ceiling. The birthday child is blindfolded and has to hit it with a stick until it bursts open and the candy spills out.
18. Nepal	In Nepal, it's traditional to smear the forehead of the birthday child with colored rice yogurt for good luck.
19. New Zealand	In New Zealand, after the birthday candles are lit, the happy birthday song is sung, very loud and often out of tune. ▪ Then the birthday person receives a clap for each year they have been alive and one for good luck.
20. Netherlands	In the Netherlands, it's a tradition to congratulate everyone (the parents, the friends, the neighbors), not just the birthday child. ▪ The birthdays of 5, 10, 15, 20, and 21 years are special, and the birthday child receives an especially large gift.

BIRTHDAYS AROUND THE WORLD

21. Nigeria	In Nigeria, the 1st, 5th, 10th, and 15th birthdays are considered special events. ▪ On these birthdays, there are huge parties with up to 100 guests or more. ▪ Often there is a feast consisting of an entire roasted cow or goat.
22. Norway	In Norway, the birthday child stands in front of the class and chooses a friend to share a little dance with, while the rest of the class sings a happy birthday song.
23. Peru	Guests at a Peruvian birthday party received two party favors. ▪ They get to bring home a bag filled with sweet goodies and a pin to mark the special party. ▪ At these parties, children almost always receive fancy paper hats.
24. Russia	In Russia, instead of a birthday cake, there's a pie with a birthday greeting carved into the crust. ▪ At a birthday party, there are clotheslines from which small gifts hang. Each kid pulls one down as a party favor.
25. Scotland	In Scotland, on their birthday, a child receives a one-pound note for each year and an additional pound for good luck. ▪ Also, the child gets a soft smack on the bottom for each year.
26. USA	In the United States, there's a theme-decorated cake with candles representing the age of the child. ▪ Everyone sings "Happy Birthday to You." ▪ The birthday child makes a wish and tries to blow out all the candles with one breath. ▪ If they succeed, then the wish will come true.

Young Achievers

1. At the age of 2, Toni Sailer (Austria) learned to ski. He later won three gold medals in a single Olympics.

2. At the age of 2, Jaylan Amor (Australia) could surf and ride big waves.

3. At the age of 3, Jacob Barnett (USA) was able to recite the alphabet forwards and backwards.

4. At the age of 4, Kim Ung Yong (Korea) could solve complicated problems in calculus.

5. At the age of 5, future mathematician William Hamilton (Ireland) learned Latin, Greek, and Hebrew.

6. At the age of 6, Joshua Beckford (England) was admitted to a program for gifted children at Oxford University, where he took certificate courses in both history and philosophy—and passed with distinction.

7. At the age of 7, Akrit Jaswal (India), successfully operated on a young girl in his native village, whose fingers had been melted together in a fire.

8. At the age of 7, Elaina Smith had her own radio show as Britain's youngest Agony Aunt advising adult listeners on their relationship problems.

9. At the age of 8, Mozart wrote his first symphony.

10. At the age of 9, Saul Kripke (USA) had read the complete works of Shakespeare.

YOUNG ACHIEVERS

11. At the age of 10, Michael Kearney (USA) graduated from college, earning a bachelor's degree in anthropology.

12. At the age of 11, Thomas Gregory (UK), swam across the English Channel. It took 11 hours and 54 minutes.

13. At the age of 12, Rubén Darío (Nicaragua) was a recognized poet.

14. At the age of 13, Jordan Romero (USA) climbed Mount Everest.

15. At the age of 14, Marsai Martin (USA), was the star and executive producer of the Hollywood film *Little*.

16. At the age of 15, Louis Braille, blind since age 3, perfected his method of raised writing.

17. At the age of 16, Lewis Clarke (UK) skied 1,123 km (698 miles) to the Geographic South Pole, as part of a two-man expedition.

18. At the age of 17, Malala Yousafzai (Pakistan) won the Noble Prize for Peace.

19. At the age of 18, Michael Sessions was elected mayor of a city in the United States.

20. At the age of 19, Oliver Crane (USA) rowed solo across the Atlantic Ocean. It took 44 days, 16 hours and 9 minutes.

21. At the age of 20, Bill Gates dropped out of Harvard and founded Microsoft.

Older Achievers

1. At the age of 85, Jessica Tandy starred in her final film, *Camilla*.

2. At the age of 86, Katherine Pelton swam the 200-meter butterfly in 3 minutes.

3. At the age of 87, Mary Baker Eddy founded the newspaper the *Christian Science Monitor*.

4. At the age of 88, Doris Travis graduated from the University of Oklahoma with a degree in history.

5. At the age of 89, Albert Schweitzer, the German-born French philosopher and medical missionary, headed a hospital in Africa.

6. At the age of 89, pianist Arthur Rubinstein gave one of his greatest performances in New York's Carnegie Hall.

7. At the age of 90, Perry Biddle was able to do a human flag, holding on to a pole with his hands and maintaining his body parallel to the ground.

8. At the age of 90, American composer Elliott Cook Carter wrote his first opera. He published more than 40 works between ages 90 and 100.

9. At the age of 90, Pablo Picasso was still producing his world-famous works of art.

10. At the age of 91, Hulda Crooks climbed Mount Whitney, the highest mountain in the continental United States.

OLDER ACHIEVERS

11. At the age of 93, Strom Thurmond, the longest-serving senator in U.S. history, won reelection after promising not to run again at age 99.

12. At the age of 94, Portuguese filmmaker Manoel de Oliveira directed the film *A Talking Picture*.

13. At the age of 94, comedian George Burns performed at a theater in New York—63 years after he first performed there.

14. At the age of 95, Nola Ochs graduated from college with a degree in general studies with an emphasis on history.

15. At the age of 96, Dorothy Geeben was mayor of the city Ocean Breeze Park.

16. At the age of 96, Gus Langner swam the 1,500-meter freestyle in 47 minutes.

17. At the age of 97, Martin Miller was still working full-time.

18. At the age of 98, artist Beatrice Wood exhibited her latest works.

19. At the age of 99, David Ray started to learn to read.

20. At the age of 100, Fauja Singh (UK) ran and finished a marathon.

21. At the age of 100, the painter known as "Grandma Moses" was still painting.

22. At the age of 101, Mary Hardison did a tandem paraglide.

Interesting People

1.	Buzz Aldrin	Edwin "Buzz" Aldrin (born 1930) is an American astronaut. ▪ On July 21, 1969, nineteen minutes after Neil Armstrong, he set foot on the moon. ▪ He was thus the second person in history to walk on the moon.
2.	Muhammad Ali	Muhammad Ali (1942–2016) was an American world champion boxer. ▪ He was known for his strong religious and political convictions; and for his clever rhymes: "I'm going to float like a butterfly and sting like a bee; his hands can't hit what his eyes can't see."
3.	Roald Amundsen	Roald Amundsen (1872–1928) was a Norwegian explorer. ▪ In 1911, he became the first man to reach the South Pole. ▪ Part of his preparation was sleeping with his windows open during the freezing Norwegian winters.
4.	André the Giant	André the Giant (1946–1993) was a French professional wrestler. ▪ He was almost 2.1 meters (7 feet) tall and weighed close to 230 kilos (500 pounds). ▪ His nickname was "Monster Eiffel Tower." ▪ He played a giant in the 1987 movie *The Princess Bride*.
5.	Ronald Biggs	Ronald Biggs (1929–2013) was a British robber. ▪ In 1963, he was part of the biggest train robbery in British history. ▪ He was caught, went to prison, escaped, and fled to Rio de Janeiro, where he married a Brazilian and became a minor celebrity, recounting his story and signing autographs.

INTERESTING PEOPLE

6.	Christiaan Barnard	Christiaan Barnard (1922–2001) was a South African heart surgeon. In December of 1967, he performed the first successful heart transplant.
7.	Christy Brown	Christy Brown (1932–1981) was an Irish author, poet, and painter. ▪ He had severe cerebral palsy. ▪ He couldn't speak or move any part of his body except his left foot, which he used to write and paint. ▪ He's famous for his autobiography *(My Left Foot)*.
8.	Miguel de Cervantes	Cervantes (1547–1616) was a Spanish writer. ▪ His most famous book was *Don Quixote de la Mancha*. ▪ An elderly gentleman goes mad and believes he is a medieval knight. ▪ In one famous adventure, he attacks windmills, believing they are evil giants.
9.	Lewis Carroll	Charles Dodgson (1832–1898), better known as Lewis Carroll, wrote *Alice in Wonderland*. ▪ A young girl follows a rabbit with a pocket watch into a hole where she meets a talking caterpillar sitting on a mushroom smoking a hookah. ▪ She also meets a Cheshire cat that can disappear leaving only its grin.
10.	Agatha Christie	Agatha Christie (1890 –1976) was an English writer of crime stories. She has sold over 4 billion books around the world
11.	James Cook	James Cook (1728–1779) was an explorer, navigator, and cartographer. ▪ In 1778 he discovered the Hawaiian Islands. ▪ On his third visit to the islands, he was killed by a mob of angry natives.

INTERESTING PEOPLE

12. Howard Carter	Howard Carter (1874–1939) was a British archaeologist. In 1922, he discovered the hidden tomb of the Egyptian Pharaoh Tutankhamun (known as "King Tut") who died over 3,300 years ago.
13. George Washington Carver	George Washington Carver (1864–1943) was an Afro-American scientist and inventor who was born a slave. He's famous for developing nearly 300 products made from peanuts, such as flour, paper, soap, shaving cream, skin lotion, laxatives, ink, and shampoo.
14. Daniel Defoe	Daniel Defoe (1660–1731) was an English author. ▪ His best known work is *Robinson Crusoe,* the story of a man who is shipwrecked on an island, where he lives for 28 years. ▪ He narrates the many things he does to survive and create a pleasant life, including making friends with a cannibal.
15. Arthur Conan Doyle	Arthur Conan Doyle (1859–1930) was a Scottish author. He's known for his short stories about the eccentric detective Sherlock Holmes. ▪ In his later years, Doyle embraced spiritualism and was a member of the Ghost Club, an organization for supernatural investigations.
16. Alberto Santos-Dumont	Alberto Santos-Dumont (1873–1932) was a Brazilian aviation pioneer who made some of the first heavier-than-air flights. ▪ In 1906, in Paris, he flew 61 meters (200 feet) at a height of 4.5 meters (15 feet). ▪ This was the world's first *public* powered flight.

INTERESTING PEOPLE

17. Thomas Edison	Thomas Edison (1847–1931) was an American inventor. Some of his many inventions include the phonograph; the first practical lightbulb; and the motion picture camera, which gave him the name "the father of motion pictures."
18. Leif Ericson	Leif Ericson (970–1029) was a Norse explorer. It's believed that he set foot on North America in what's now Newfoundland, Canada, 500 years before Columbus.
19. James Fixx	James Fixx (1932–1984) wrote the 1977 best-selling book *The Complete Book of Running*, which helped start the American fitness revolution by popularizing jogging.
20. Anne Frank	Anne Frank (1929–1945) was a young Jewish girl who died in the Holocaust. ▪ Her family spent two years hiding from the Nazis, but they were found, and Anne died in a concentration camp. ▪ Her diary has been published in over 70 languages.
21. Yuri Gagarin	Yuri Gagarin (1934–1968) was a Russian cosmonaut (astronaut). On April 12, 1961, he became the first human to orbit the earth.
22. John Griffin	John Howard Griffin, (1920–1980), was a white American author who temporarily altered the pigment of his skin in order to experience firsthand the life of a black man in the South of the United States. ▪ His book *Black like Me* (1961) detailed countless incidents of discrimination, hatred, suspicion, and hostility.

INTERESTING PEOPLE

23. Stephen Hawking	Stephen Hawking (1942–2018) was a British scientist known for his work on the origin of the universe. At the age of 21, he was diagnosed with ALS, a motor-neuron disease that left him completely paralyzed. He is also famous for his fortitude and positive outlook.
24. Harry Houdini	Harry Houdini (1874 –1926) was a Hungarian-born American magician and escape artist. He was famous for his ability to escape from handcuffs, straitjackets, jail cells, and even boxes that had been nailed shut and thrown into a river.
25. Boris Karloff	Boris Karloff (1887–1969) was an English actor. ▪ He's known for his roles in the first horror movies. ▪ In 1931 he played the monster Frankenstein, and in 1932 he starred in the film *The Mummy*.
26. Ray Kroc	Ray Kroc (1902–1984) was an American entrepreneur. In 1961 he bought a small chain of restaurants from the two McDonald brothers and turned it into the McDonald's fast-food Corporation, keeping the original name.
27. Helen Keller	Helen Keller (1880–1968) was an American author, educator, and crusader for the handicapped. She was the first blind and death person to earn a bachelor of arts degree.
28. Charles Lindbergh	Charles Lindbergh (1902–1974) was a pioneering American airplane pilot. ▪ In 1927, he made the first solo non-stop flight across the Atlantic Ocean, flying from New York to Paris in 33 hours.

INTERESTING PEOPLE

29. Rosa Parks	Rosa Parks (1913–2005) was an African-American civil rights activist. ▪ In 1955, on a public bus, she refused to give up her seat to a white passenger and was arrested. ▪ This led to a black boycott of the city buses and helped launch the US Civil Rights Movement.
30. Pelé	Pelé (born 1940) is a former Brazilian football (soccer) player. ▪ At the age of 17, Pelé helped lead Brazil to win the 1958 World Cup. ▪ He's considered one of the best, if not the best, player in the history of football.
31. Steven Spielberg	Steven Spielberg (born 1946) is an American filmmaker. Some of his best-known films include *Jaws,* the *Indiana Jones* films, *E.T., The Color Purple, Jurassic Park, Hook,* and *Amistad.*
32. Mary Shelley	Mary Shelley (1797–1851) was an English author known for writing the novel *Frankenstein.* ▪ In this book, a mad scientist, Victor Frankenstein, creates a man from the body parts of dead men and brings it to life.
33. Jerry Siegel	Jerry Siegel (1914 –1996), was an American comic book writer. In 1939, he created Superman in collaboration with his friend Joe Shuster (1914–1992).
34. Jimmy Wales	Jimmy Wales (born 1966) is an Amerian-British Internet entrepreneur. ▪ In 2001, together with Larry Sanger, he founded the online encyclopedia Wikipedia. ▪ There are now Sister Projects that include a dictionary, a simple English Wikipedia, a collection of quotations, a free media repository, and free textbooks.

Curious Deaths

1. The English Duke of Clarence reportedly died when his brother, Richard III, had him drowned in a barrel of wine. The year: 1478.

2. The English philosopher Francis Bacon (1561–1626) wanted to discover whether snow would delay putrefaction of a dead body. He stopped his carriage, got out, bought a hen, killed it, stuffed it with snow, caught a cold, and died.

3. In 1884, Allan Pinkerton, the founder of the Pinkerton Detective Agency, slipped on the pavement, bit his tongue, and died of gangrene.

4. In 1927, Isadora Duncan (1877–1927), a famous American dancer, was riding in a sports car when her long scarf became entangled in the rear wheel, hurling her from the car, breaking her neck.

5. Alexander, the king of Greece from 1917 to 1920, was bitten by a pet monkey and died from blood poisoning.

6. A 39-year-old man in Germany who had been drinking told his friends, "Now, I'm going to kill myself." He went outside, lifted the cover of a sewer, and jumped in headfirst.

7. In 1903, a man from Saint Louis took his first bath in 20 years, and it killed him. It didn't help that he was scrubbed with a broom.

8. According to legend, one night, the famous Chinese poet Li Po was quite drunk in a canoe. He saw a reflection of the moon in the water, tried to kiss it, fell into the water, and drowned. The year: 762 A.D.

CURIOUS DEATHS

9. A man from Bavaria (now Austria) had an exceptionally long beard. One day he stepped on it, lost his balance, fell down the stairs, and died. The year: 1567

10. In 1989, a man from Denmark laughed so hard at a scene in the film *A Fish Called Wanda* that he had a fatal heart attack.

11. In 1771, Adolf Frederick (1710–1771), the King of Sweden, died of indigestion after eating a meal of lobster, caviar, sauerkraut, smoked herring, champagne, and 14 servings of his favorite dessert.

12. In 1979, a worker at a Ford Motor plant became the first person known to be killed by a robot when the arm of a factory robot struck him in the head while he was repairing a malfunction.

13. In 1982, a man in Arizona fired his shotgun at a giant cactus in the desert. The shots caused a 7-meter (23-foot) section of the cactus to fall on him, and he was crushed to death.

14. A 24-year-old man in England died from cardiac arrest in a movie theater while looking for his dropped cell phone. His head had become wedged under the electronic footrest of a seat.

15. In 2016, a 55-year-old woman was fatally stabbed in the chest by a beach umbrella blown by a sudden strong wind.

16. In 1982, a 26-year-old man was playing golf with some friends. ▪ After making a bad shot, he became angry and threw his club against a golf cart. ▪ The club broke, rebounded, and stabbed him in the throat.

17. In 1924, British newspapers reported the bizarre case of a man who apparently committed suicide while asleep. He woke up to discover he had slit his own throat.

Death by Stupidity

1. A drunk security guard at a Moscow bank asked a fellow worker to stab his bulletproof vest to see if it would protect him against a knife attack. It didn't.

2. A man from the state of Alabama (USA) died from rattlesnake bites while playing snake catch with a friend.

3. The lead singer of the '70s band Chicago playfully pointed a gun at his head. His last words were: "Don't worry. It's not loaded."

4. A woman from Florida (USA) with a genius IQ of 189 was so worried about dying from stomach cancer that she drank 15 liters (4 gallons) of water a day. She died at the age of 29 of kidney failure.

5. In 1983, a woman in California was arrested for shoplifting. She swore she would hold her breath until she turned blue if the police didn't release her. They didn't, she did, and she died.

6. In 1808, two men from Paris fought a duel with muskets in hot-air balloons. One man, wisely, shot the other man's balloon, and he died from the fall.

7. In 1990, a man who was an expert kayaker thought he could kayak over Niagara Falls. He could, but only once.

8. In 1871, a lawyer argued that his client shouldn't be convicted of murder because the victim might have accidentally shot himself. Demonstrating how, the lawyer accidentally shot himself and died, proving his point.

DEATH BY STUPIDITY

9. In 1993, a lawyer wanted to demonstrate that a building's windows were "unbreakable." He threw himself against the window. ▪ The window didn't break but popped out of its frame, and he fell 24 floors to his death.

10. A 32-year-old man plugged his charger into an extension cord and rested it on his chest while using the phone in the bathtub. When the charger touched the water, he received severe burns and died of heart failure.

11. In 2018, a man in India was driving home from a wedding. He saw what appeared to be an injured bear and decided to get a selfie with it. When he got close, the bear, which wasn't injured, attacked and killed him.

12. In 2005, a 28-year-old man from South Korea played video games for 50 hours straight, taking only brief breaks to go to the bathroom or nap. He collapsed and died from exhaustion, dehydration, and heart failure.

13. In 1912, a tailor in France created a coat that could also work as a parachute. Confident that his invention would work, he calmly stepped off a platform at the top of the Eiffel Tower and plunged to his death.

14. In 2018, a 21-year-old man was on a party cruise in the Boston Harbor. He decided to show off his physical skills by doing handstands (vertical pushups) on the railing of the boat. He lost his balance, fell overboard, and drowned.

Funny Tombstones

1. I told you I was sick.

2. Now I know something you don't.

3. Here I lie, but don't you cry. For one day too, you will die.

4. The doctor will see you soon. *(on the grave of a doctor)*

5. This is not what I had in mind when I said, "Over my dead body."

6. The shop said the brakes were fixed right this time.

7. He never killed a man that didn't need killing. *(1887, on the grave of a cowboy)*

8. Uncle Walter loved to spend. He had no money in the end. But with many a whisky and many a wife. He really did enjoy his life.

9. Here lies an atheist. All dressed up and no place to go.

10. Here lies Fred the dentist … in the biggest cavity he ever filled.

11. Here lies the body of Jonathan Blake. Stepped on the gas instead of the brake.

12. Here lies an honest lawyer and that is Strange. *(on the grave of John Strange)*

13. Here lies Ezekial Aikle. Age 102. The good die young.

Bizarre Laws

1. In the UK, it's illegal to fire a cannon within 270 meters (300 yards) of someone's house.

2. In Denmark, it's illegal to give your baby a weird or unconventional name.

3. In Florida (USA) it's illegal for a divorced or a widowed woman to skydive on a Sunday afternoon.

4. In Turin, Italy, by law dog owners must take their dogs on a walk at least three times a day.

5. In Hong Kong, there's a law that allows a wife to kill her husband if she finds him cheating. However, she must kill him with her bare hands.

6. In Iowa (USA), it's illegal for a man with a mustache to kiss a woman in public.

7. In Kentucky (USA), a woman cannot remarry the same man more than three times.

8. In Florida (USA), it's illegal to sell your children.

9. In Chico, California, it's illegal to build or detonate a nuclear weapon.

10. In Victoria, Australia, only a qualified electrician is allowed to change a light bulb.

11. In Scotland, being drunk on a cow is against the law.

BIZARRE LAWS

12. In France, it's illegal to offend the heads of state by naming your pig after them.

13. In a small town in Russia, it's illegal to drive a dirty car.

14. In Australia, it's illegal to intentionally disrupt a wedding.

15. In China, reincarnation is illegal without the government's permission.

16. In Chicago, it's illegal to fish while sitting on a giraffe's neck.

17. In Samoa, it's illegal to forget your wife's birthday.

18. In Kentucky (USA), carrying ice cream cones in your pocket is illegal.

19. In Milan, Italy, by law everyone must always smile, except during funerals or visiting a hospital.

20. In New Zealand, there's a law that states you cannot fly with a rooster in a hot air balloon.

21. In England, it's illegal to flag down a taxi if you have the plague.

22. In Switzerland, it's illegal to ski down a mountain while reciting poetry.

23. During Sweden's long hours of winter darkness, it's illegal to complain that you wish it were sunny.

24. In Denmark, it's a crime for a man to say to his wife that she's uglier than her mother.

Strange Lawsuits

1. A man in Pennsylvania (USA) sued the Devil. ▪ He claimed that Satan had placed obstacles in his life that caused his downfall. ▪ The court dismissed the suit saying the defendant (Satan) didn't reside in the state.

2. A man sued his church when, after three years, he didn't receive the "blessings, benefits and rewards" the pastor had said would come if he donated 10% of his wealth to the church.

3. A 24-year-old man sued his parents for "parental malpractice." He claimed they had been such bad parents that he would need psychiatric care for the rest of his life.

4. A 41-year-old accountant in California was upset when a girl he had asked out for dinner didn't show up. He sued her for "breaking an oral contract" He asked for $38 in compensation. The judge ruled against him.

5. A woman filed a $250,000 lawsuit when she learned that she had been praying at the wrong grave for 17 years. When workers opened the grave to move the coffin to another plot, they discovered it wasn't her husband's coffin.

6. A man sued the Coors Beer Company and a local tavern for $2 million. He claimed they had caused him to become an alcoholic because they had failed to warn him that beer is an intoxicating beverage.

7. A policeman once tried to sue Starbucks for $750,000 after he accidentally spilled a free cup of hot coffee on his lap.

STRANGE LAWSUITS

8. A woman whose twin sister died in an airplane disaster sued the airline for injuries even though she wasn't in the crash. She claimed her injuries were the result of "extrasensory empathy" which is common among identical twins.

9. A police officer had a stroke while guarding the mask of a famous Egyptian pharaoh when it was on display in San Francisco. He claimed he deserved compensation because he was a victim of the famous Curse of King Tut.

10. A woman ran up a $350,000 debt gambling at a hotel in Las Vegas. She sued the hotel to have her debt cancelled, alleging that the hotel had been negligent because it didn't inform her that she was an incompetent gambler.

11. A 69-year-old Dutchman wanted to legally change his age. He felt his real age was affecting his possibility of finding a job, as well as his chances of success on Tinder, a popular dating app.

12. A 37-year-old man sued the woman he took to a movie. He was offended because she spent the whole time texting. She agreed to pay him the money for the movie ticket if he left her alone.

13. A university in the Netherlands expelled a student who never wore shoes and never washed his feet, saying the odor was distracting to other students. A judge ruled that smelly feet were not a valid reason to expel a student.

14. A forty-four-year-old man decided to sue his employer because he felt his job was too boring, and it was causing him to become depressed.

Stupid Thieves

1. A man was arrested for stealing a pair of size 10 ½ tan hiking boots. When he wore those boots to his trial, he was convicted and sent to jail.

2. A man and two female accomplices were caught shoplifting. Unfortunately, they chose to shoplift on the day the store was hosting a convention of store detectives.

3. A man broke into a home. ▪ When the woman told him that she didn't have any cash, he told her to write him a check. ▪ She asked what name she should put on the check. ▪ He gave her his name and was arrested several hours later.

4. A man in England robbed a store. ▪ To hide his identity, he wore his full-face motorcycle helmet as a mask. ▪ Unfortunately, he didn't remember that his name was on the front of the helmet in big letters.

5. A man was charged with stealing a woman's purse. ▪ He decided to act as his own attorney at the trial. ▪ While cross-examining the victim, he incredibly asked: "Did you get a good look at my face when I took your purse?"

6. Three men were trying to steal a pickup truck. ▪ When the owner appeared, they ran and climbed over a fence, hoping to escape. ▪ But, unfortunately they chose the fence surrounding the property of a prison.

7. A man in Brazil tried to break into a bar through the roof. ▪ He slipped, fell, and accidently shot himself in the foot. ▪ He then went straight home. ▪ The trail of blood dripping from his foot led the police right to his door.

STUPID THIEVES

8. A shoplifter was arrested after he left a liquor store with a bottle of vodka. ▪ It wasn't hard to find him. ▪ He had asked the clerk out on a date and had left her his name and phone number, in case she wanted to call him. ▪ She didn't, but the police did.

9. Thieves broke into a home and stole three jars of cocaine. ▪ They took them home and snorted the contents. ▪ Only later they discovered that the jars were urns. ▪ They had been snorting the cremated remains of the victim's husband and their two dogs.

10. A woman was stopped by the police for drunk driving. Trying to be helpful, she offered this information to the police: "My husband is right behind me, and he's even drunker than I am."

11. A good Samaritan noticed an elderly man being robbed, so he jumped in and punched the thief. The thief was so upset that he called the police to complain.

12. A store agreed to take back a printer from a dissatisfied customer. Then the clerk noticed some work the customer had forgotten to remove from the machine: counterfeit bills.

13. After a man kicked in the front door of a home at 3:30 a.m., the resident fled and called the police. ▪ When they arrived, they found the intruder hadn't stolen anything. ▪ But he was in the bathroom, enjoying a warm bath.

14. A man suffered a heart attack and thinking he was going to die confessed to a murder he had committed 17 years earlier. ▪ Only he didn't die. ▪ He was arrested and sentenced to life in prison.

Unusual Books

1. *The Joy of Chickens*
2. *Teach your Wife to Be a Widow*
3. *Old Age: Its Causes and Prevention*
4. *Practical Candle Burning: Spells and Rituals for Every Purpose*
5. *Across Europe by Kangaroo*
6. *Carnivorous Butterflies*
7. *Do-it-yourself Coffins: For Pets and People*
8. *The Zombie Guide: Complete Protection from the Living Dead*
9. *How to Be Happy though Married*
10. *How to Be Pretty though Plain*
11. *How to Become a Schizophrenic*
12. *How to Rob Banks without Violence*
13. *How to Start Your Own Country*
14. *How to Talk to Your Cat about Gun Safety*

Crazy Song Titles

1. You're the Reason Our Kids Are Ugly
2. If the Phone Doesn't Ring, It's Me
3. How Can I Miss You, If You Won't Go Away?
4. I Like Bananas Because They Have No Bones
5. I Scream, You Scream, We All Scream for Ice Cream
6. I Keep Forgetting that I Forgot about You
7. Mama Get Your Hammer—There's a Fly on Baby's Head
8. I'm So Miserable without You—It's Just like Having You Around
9. Tiptoe through the Tulips
10. Who's Gonna Take Out the Garbage When I'm Dead and Gone?
11. Come after Breakfast, Bring Your Lunch, and Leave before Suppertime
12. If You Can't Live without Me, Why Aren't You Dead Yet?
13. How Could You Believe Me When I Said I Loved You When You Know I've Been a Liar All My Life?
14. I've Got Those Wake Up Seven Thirty, Wash Your Ears, They're Dirty, Eat Your Eggs and Oatmeal Rush to School Blues

Superstitions

1. A black cat crossing your path is unlucky.

2. If you hear dogs howling at night, it means that someone is going to die.

3. If you walk under a ladder, it will bring bad luck.

4. If your palm feels itchy, it means that money will come your way.

5. If you break a mirror, you will have seven years of bad luck.

6. Friday the 13th is considered an unlucky day.

7. If you spill salt, toss some over your left shoulder to avoid bad luck.

8. If the first butterfly you see in the year is white, you will have good luck all year.

9. It's bad luck to leave a house through a different door than the one used to come in.

10. If you catch a falling leaf on the first day of autumn, you won't catch a cold all winter.

11. Dropping an umbrella on the floor means that there will be a murder in the house.

12. If the groom drops the wedding band during the ceremony, the marriage is doomed.

SUPERSTITIONS

13. You should never start a trip on Friday, or you will meet misfortune.

14. It's bad luck to open an umbrella indoors.

15. Knock on wood for good luck to continue.

16. The number 13 is unlucky.

17. The number 7 is lucky.

18. Putting a hat on the bed will bring bad luck.

19. It's bad luck for the groom to see the bride on the wedding day before the ceremony.

20. If you make a wish and then blow out all the candles on your birthday cake, your wish will be granted.

21. If you step on a crack in the sidewalk, you will break your mother's back.

22. Cross your fingers to avoid bad luck and help a wish to come true.

23. Garlic protects from evil spirits and vampires.

24. If your ears are burning, someone is talking about you.

25. A frog brings good luck to the house it enters.

26. Looking at the moon over the right shoulder brings good luck.

Curious Inventions

1. *Tomatan* is a wearable robot that sits on your head and feeds you tomatoes directly into your mouth as you walk.

2. A *nose stylus* allows you to keep a hand free for other tasks while you use it to operate your phone.

3. A *mustache shield* invented in 1876 was designed to keep your mustache out of the way when you're eating or drinking.

4. *Grass flip flops* give you the sensation of walking on grass.

5. The *coffee mug iron* lets you enjoy your morning coffee and iron your clothes with the same hand.

6. *Glow in the dark toilet paper* looks perfectly normal until the lights go out. Then, all of sudden, it's bright glowing green.

7. *Drop wipes* are car wipes that are specifically designed to remove bird poop from the exterior of your car.

8. The *Kohler intelligent toilet* allows you to check the news, find out the weather, or order groceries while seated on its heated seat.

9. *FoldiMate* is a robotic laundry folder that will fold a load of 25 laundry items in less than 5 minutes.

10. The *Kiki Pet Robot* is perfect for the person who wants a pet but doesn't want the hassle. This "pet" will even sing or dance if it senses its owner is down in the dumps.

When was it Invented?

Air conditioner	1902		Cell phone	1973
Airplane	1903		Coca Cola	1886
Aluminum can	1958		Contact lenses	1887
Apple computer	1976		Dishwasher	1886
Aspirin	1897		DVD	1995
Atomic bomb	1945		E-mail	1971
Ball-point pen	1938		Frozen food	1924
Band-aide	1920		Glasses	1284
Barcode	1951		Glue	1750
Battery	1800		Guitar	1779
Bikini	1946		Hamburger	1920
CD	1982		Hot dog	1852

WHEN WAS IT INVENTED?

Instant coffee	1890	Pop-up toaster	1919
Internet	1969	Post-it notes	1974
Jeans	1873	Potato chips	1853
Laser	1960	Rubber eraser	1770
Microscope	1590	Sandwich	1762
Microwave	1946	Scotch tape	1930
Mouse	1964	Shopping cart	1937
Neon sign	1910	Stapler	1866
Parachute	1783	Talking films	1927
Parking meter	1935	Tin can	1810
PC computer	1981	Toilet	1775
Pencil	1795	Toilet paper	1857
Piano	1770	Xerox	1963

Unsolved Mysteries

1.	The Mary Celeste	In 1872, the *Mary Celeste*, an American sailing ship, was found floating, unoccupied, in the middle of the Atlantic Ocean. ▪ The lifeboats were missing, but the ship was in perfect condition, and there were ample provisions on board. ▪ The captain, his family, and the crew were never seen again.
2.	Stonehenge	Stonehenge is a prehistoric monument located in southern England. ▪ It consists of a ring of massive standing stones. ▪ Each stone is around 4 meters (13 feet) high, 2.1 meters (seven feet) wide, and weighs around 25 tons.
3.	Pyramid of Giza	The Great Pyramid of Giza used around 2.3 million stone blocks, each one weighing more than 2 tons. ▪ How they cut, moved, and fit these blocks is a mystery. ▪ Other mysteries include the fact that the pyramid's dimensions are related to the circumference of the earth at the equator and to the distance from the earth to the sun.
4.	Easter Island	Easter Island is famous for its nearly 1,000 massive stone statues called Moai. ▪ On the average, the statues are 4 meters (13 feet) tall and weigh around 13 tons. ▪ They have unusually large heads with broad elongated noses and rectangular ears. ▪ Nobody knows the purpose of the statues, nor how they were transported across the island.

UNSOLVED MYSTERIES

5.	Stone spheres in Costa Rica	In the 1930s, around 300 stone balls were discovered in the jungle of Costa Rica. ▪ The largest weighed 16 tons. ▪ Nobody knows how primitive people with primitive tools could have made them so smooth and so almost perfectly round.
6.	Nazca lines	The Nazca lines are designs that were etched into the ground in the coastal plain of Peru between 400 and 600 A.D. ▪ There are straight lines 48 kilometers (30 miles) in length, and immense figures depicting animals and geometric shapes, which can only be seen from the air. ▪ Nobody knows how and for what purpose these lines and figures were created.
7.	Jack the Ripper	In 1888, five prostitutes in London were viciously murdered. ▪ The killer slashed the victims, cut open the abdomen, and removed organs, giving him the nickname "Jack the Ripper." ▪ To this day no one knows who the ripper was.
8.	Shroud of Turin	The shroud of Turin is a linen cloth bearing the image of a man who apparently died of crucifixion. ▪ Some consider it to be the burial shroud of Jesus. ▪ No one has yet been able to explain how the image became imprinted on the shroud.
9.	Spontaneous combustion	In Galway, Ireland, 76-year-old Michael Faherty was found burned to death at his home in December 2010. The coroner concluded Faherty's death was a case of spontaneous human combustion—a human being catching fire with no apparent cause.

UNSOLVED MYSTERIES

10. Extinction of the dinosaurs	Dinosaurs roamed the earth for about 135 million years. ▪ But about 65 million years ago they became extinct. ▪ One theory is that a giant asteroid struck the earth. ▪ Another theory is that volcanic eruptions sent up a giant dust cloud blocking out the sunlight, which led to massive changes in climate. ▪ Nobody knows what really happened.
11. Tunguska event	On the morning of June 30, 1908, a giant explosion, known as the Tunguska event, shook central Siberia. ▪ Witnesses described seeing a fireball in the sky as bright as the sun. ▪ The explosion leveled 80 million trees. ▪ It's thought that a either a meteor or a comet exploded a couple of miles above the ground.
12. Reincarnation	A three-year-old named Lee told his parents: **(1)** he was really born on June 26; **(2)** his middle name was Coe; **(3)** he used to write movies; **(4)** he had a daughter named Jennifer; **(5)** and that in a previous life he had died at age forty-eight. ▪ They later discovered that the author of the screen play for the movie *Gone with the Wind* was Sidney Coe Howard, who was born on June 26, had a daughter Jennifer, and had died at age forty-eight.
13. Prophetic dreams	The author Mark Twain had a prophetic dream in which he saw his brother in a coffin. ▪ His brother died only weeks later in a boating accident. ▪ He also predicted that his own death would coincide with the return of Halley's comet, which is exactly what happened in 1910.

UNSOLVED MYSTERIES

14. Bermuda triangle	The Bermuda triangle is an area of water in the North Atlantic Ocean in which a large number of planes and boats have gone missing in mysterious circumstances. • Explanations have included bad weather, alien abductions, and entering another dimension or universe.
15. Disembodied feet	In August of 2007, a disembodied human foot, still in an Adidas tennis shoe, washed up on a beach near Vancouver, British Columbia. • Since then a total of 14 feet, usually in sneakers, have been found on the beaches of British Columbia. • None of the human remains showed signs of trauma.

Appendices

1. Animals **136**

2. Countries **137**

3. People **139**

4. Vocabulary for *The Global Table* **143**

5. Vocabulary for *Breakfast around the World* **144**

Appendix 1: Animals

Except for *giant weta* and *kori bustard*, these all have articles in *Simple English Wikipedia*.

anaconda	giant weta	penguin
ant	giraffe	pig
bat	goliath bird eating spider	polar bear
bear	goliath frog	python
bee hummingbird	gorilla	rhinoceros
blue whale	Great Dane	sea turtle
bulldog	hippopotamus	seal
camel	horse	skunk
cat	howler monkey	sloth
chameleon	hummingbird	Saint Bernard
cheetah	Irish setter	whale shark
chimpanzee	kangaroo	woodpecker
cockroach	kori bustard	
crocodile	leopard	
dinosaur	lion	
dog	lizard	
eagle	lobster	
electric eel	mouse	
elephant	octopus	
flying fox bat	okapi	
frog	ostrich	
giant panda	owl	

Appendix 2: Countries

All of these countries have articles in *Simple English Wikipedia*.

Afghanistan	Denmark	Ireland
Argentina	Dominican Republic	Israel
Australia	Ecuador	Italy
Austria	Egypt	Jamaica
Bali	El Salvador	Japan
Bangladesh	England	Jordan
Belgium	Ethiopia	Kenya
Bolivia	Fiji	Korea
Borneo	Finland	Kuwait
Botswana	France	Libya
Brazil	Georgia	Luxembourg
Brunei	Germany	Malaysia
Bulgaria	Ghana	Mauritania
Cambodia	Greece	Mexico
Canada	Greenland	Morocco
Chile	Guatemala	Mozambique
China	Hungary	Nepal
Colombia	Iceland	Netherlands
Costa Rica	India	New Zealand
Croatia	Indonesia	Nigeria
Cuba	Iran	Norway
Czech Republic	Iraq	Pakistan

APPENDIX 2: COUNTRIES

Panama
Papua New Guinea
Paraguay
Peru
Philippines
Poland
Portugal
Puerto Rico
Romania
Russia
Scotland
Spain
Sweden
Switzerland
Syria
Taiwan
Tanzania
Thailand
Turkey
Uganda
Ukraine
United States
Venezuela
Vietnam
Zambia
Zanzibar

Appendix 3: People

Every person in this appendix has an article in *Wikipedia*. Those marked by an asterisk* also have an article in *Simple English Wikipedia*. The names have been alphabetized by the first name, which will facilitate any Internet searches.

Abraham Lincoln*	Arthur Conan Doyle*	Britney Spears*
Adolf Frederick	Arthur Lintgen	Buzz Aldrin*
Agatha Christie*	Arthur Rubinstein*	Caesar*
Alain Robert	Ashrita Furman	Cervantes (Miguel) *
Alan Eustace	Babis Bizas	Chandra B. Dangi*
Albert Einstein*	Baden Powell*	Charles Darwin*
Albert Schweitzer*	Balamurali Ambati	Charles Dickens*
Alberto Santos Dumont*	Barack Obama*	Charles Lindbergh*
Alex Mullen	Barney Smith-artist*	Charles Millar
Alexander of Greece	Beatrice Wood	Charles Schulz*
Alexander the Great*	Beethoven*	Charlie Chaplin*
Allan Pinkerton	Bela Lugosi*	Christiaan Barnard
Aloha Wanderwell	Benito Mussolini*	Christopher Gluck
Amy Lowell	Benjamin Franklin*	Christy Brown
André the Giant*	Bill Gates*	Claude Monet*
Aneta Florczyk	Billy McCrary	Clyde Tombaugh*
Angelababy	Blackbeard*	Daniel B. Smith*
Anne Frank*	Bob Hope*	Daniel Defoe
Anne Parrish	Bobby Leach	Daniel Radcliffe*
Ariana Grande*	Boris Karloff*	Daniel Tammet
Art Fry	Boston Strangler	Dawn Brooke

APPENDIX 3: PEOPLE

Diamond Jim Brady
Doris Travis
Dorothy Geeben
Douglas Fairbanks*
Ed Whitlock*
Edgar Cayce*
Edmund Hillary*
Elliott Cook Carter
Emilio Scotto
Emily Rosa
Emma Roberts*
Erik the Red*
Ethel Granger
Evil Knievel*
Fauja Singh*
Florence Green*
Francis Bacon*
Frank Zappa*
Franky Zapata
Fred Baur
Fred Hale Sr.
Frederica Cook
Frederick the Great*
Gary Gilmore*
Geoffrey Capes

George Burns*
George Ferris Junior
George Freeth
George Meegan
George Speck
George Washington Carver*
George Washington*
Gerard de Nerval
Grandma Moses
Groucho Marx
Guillem de Cabestany
Hadji Ali
Handel*
Hans Langseth
Harry Houdini*
Harry Truman*
Heini Koivuniemi
Heinrich Heine*
Helen Keller*
Henri Matisse*
Henrik Ibsen*
Hetty Green
Hitler*
Howard Carter
Hulda Crooks

Isaac Newton*
Isadora Duncan*
Ivan the Terrible*
Ivy Baldwin
J. K. Rowling*
Jack the Ripper*
James Cook*
James Fixx
James Franco*
Jeane Dixon*
Jeanne Calment*
Jeff Bezos*
Jennifer Aniston*
Jerry Siegel*
Jessica Tandy*
Jigoro Kano
Jimmy Wales*
Joe Shuster
Johanna Quaas
John F. Kennedy*
John Glenn*
John Griffin Howard
John Lennon*
John Paul Getty*
Johnny Depp*

APPENDIX 3: PEOPLE

Jon Minnoch	Maarten de Jonge	Nadya Suleman*
Jordan Romero	Maggie Kuhn	Napoleon*
Joseph Aiuppa	Malala Yousafzai*	Neil Armstrong*
Joseph Henry Green	Manoel de Oliveira*	Nick Vujicic
Juan Montoya	Marco Polo*	Nicole Kidman*
Karl Benz*	Mark Twain*	Nola Ochs
Ken Dodd*	Marlene Dietrich*	Oliver Crane
Kevin Costner*	Marsai Martin	Oscar Wilde*
Kim Peek*	Mary Baker Eddy*	P. G. Wodehouse
Kim Ung-yong*	Mary Shelley*	Pablo Picasso*
Larry Walters*	Matthew Hall	Pauline Musters
Leif Ericsson*	Maya Gabeira	Pelé*
Leila Denmark*	Megan Fox*	Philippe Petit*
Leona Helmsley*	Mel Gibson*	Pink*
Leonardo da Vinci*	Michael Faherty	Plennie Wingo
Lewis Carroll*	Michael Jordan*	Rachel McAdams*
Li Po*	Michael Kearney	Ray kroc*
Liew Thow Lin	Michael Sessions	Richard Blechynden
Lionel Messi*	Michel Lotito	Richard Feynman*
Louis Braille*	Mick Jagger*	Rigoberto Hernandez
Louis Lassen	Molière*	Roald Amundsen*
Louis Pasteur*	Mother Teresa*	Robert Wadlow*
Louis VI*	Mozart*	Ronald Biggs*
Lucia Zarate	Muhammad Ali*	Rosa Parks*
Luis Garavito	Nadia Comaneci*	Roy Sullivan

APPENDIX 3: PEOPLE

Rubén Darío*
Saint Nicholas*
Salvador Dali*
Samantha Larson
Samuel Colt
Sarah Bernhardt*
Saul kripke
Seal (singer) *
Shakespeare*
Shakuntala Devi*
Shania Twain*
Sheryl Crow*
Spencer Silver
Stephen Hawking*
Steve Jobs*
Steven Spielberg*
Strom Thurmond*
Suresh Joachim
Sydney Coe Howard
Tatum O'Neal*
Taylor Swift*
Ted Coombs
Tenzing Norgay*
Theodore Roosevelt*
Thomas Edison*

Thomas Gregory
Tim FitzHigham
Toni Sailer
Truman Capote*
Usain Bolt*
Van Gogh*
Victoria Van Meter
Vinay Bhat
Walter Raleigh*
Wasantha Soysa
Wilhelm Rontgen*
William Harvey*
William Kemmler*
Wilson Mizner
Winston Churchill*
Yoko Ono*
Yuichiro Miura
Yuri Gagarin*
Zeng Jinlian
Ziad Fasah

Appendix 4: Vocabulary for *The Global Table*

baked	juice	roasted
beans	lamb	sauce
beef	lemon	savory
beets	lime	seafood
blended	liver	seasoned with
boiled	lungs	sheep
cassava	marinated	side dish
casserole	meat	smoked sausages
cheese	mushrooms	soup
chocolate	mutton	sour cream
citrus	noodles	spices
clay oven	nuts	spicy
collard greens	oatmeal	spongy
crêpe	olives	stew
dollop	onions	stir-fried
eggplant	pancakes	stomach
filling	paprika	stuffed with
flatbread	parsley	sweet peppers
fried	pastries	thick
goat	pickled cabbage	thin
gray	pork	to scoop
ground pork	potatoes	toasted
ham	preserves	tongue
heart	raisins	topped with
jelly	raw fish	vegetables

Appendix 5: Vocabulary for *Breakfast around the World*

anchovies	hearty breakfast	potatoes
apple syrup	honey	rice
avocado	hot sauce	rolls
bacon	hummus	rye bread
baked beans	jam	salami
bittersweet chocolate	lamb	sausage
boiled eggs	made with	scrambled eggs
butter	mangoes	seaweed
cheeses	maple syrup	sliced cucumbers
chocolate spread	mashed plantains	soup
coconut milk	melted into	spaghetti
cold cuts	minced meat	spicy
creamy broth	miso soup	sprinkles
crumpets	mortadella	stale bread
Danish pastries	mushrooms	steamed milk
dates	olives	topped with
deep-fried	pancakes	strong coffee
falafel	papaya	sweet rolls
flatbread	passion fruit	to soak up
fried pork	pâté	toast
full breakfast	patty (patties)	topped with
grated potatoes	peanuts	traditional
grilled tomato	pickles	tropical
ham	pineapple	typically
hash browns	pita bread	yogurt

Resources

Books

Armchair Reader: Vitally Useless Information. Lincolnwood, Illinois: Publications International/West Side Publishing, 2010. (There are many *Armchair Reader* books full of trivia and strange facts.)

Botham, Noel. *The Book of Useless Information.* New York: penguin/perigee, 2006. (There are many books in this "useless information" series.)

Fenster, Bob. *Duh! The Stupid History of the Human Race.* Kansas City: Andrews McMeel publishing, 2003.

Guinness Book of World Records. (published yearly)

Lloyd, John, et al. *1,227 Facts to Blow Your Socks Off.* London: Faber and Faber, 2012.

Lloyd, John, et al. *1,339 Facts to Make Your Jaw Drop.* London: Faber and Faber, 2013.

Mooney, Julie. *Ripley's Believe It or Not Encyclopedia of the Bizarre.* New York: Black Dog & Leventhal Publishers, 2005.

National Geographic Kids. A search on Amazon or any other book dealer will come up with a multitude of great books that National Geographic produces for kids.

Scholastic Book of World Records. New York: Scholastic Inc. (published yearly)

Siegel, Alice. and Margo McLoone. *The Blackbirch Kid's Almanac of Geography.* Woodbridge, CT: Blackbirch Press, 2000.

The World Almanac 5,001 Incredible Facts for Kids on Nature, Science, and People. New York: Skyhorse Publishing, World Almanac Books, 2020.

Internet Resources

Dictionaries	dictionary.cambridge.org (I suggest choosing the Learner's Dictionary. You have a choice of British or American English.) ldoceonline.com *(Longman Dictionary of Contemporary English)* merriam-webster.com
Pronunciation help	inogolo.com text-to-speech.imtranslator.net
Encyclopedias for adults and young adults	britannica.com en.wikipedia.org (for the English version)
Encyclopedias and facts for kids	academickids.com ducksters.com factmonster.com factsjustforkids.com kids.kiddle.co (great searchable kids' encyclopedia) simple.wikipedia.org
General fun facts	factslegend.org fun-facts.org.uk justfunfacts.com ohfact.com thefactsite.com top5ofanything.com
Animals	sciencekids.co.nz (see "facts—animal facts") thefactsite.com/animals/

INTERNET RESOURCES

Natural wonders	matadornetwork.com/trips/many-39-natural-wonders-world/ triponzy.com/blog/best-natural-wonders-of-the-world/ cnn.com/travel/article/natural-wonder-bucket-list/index.html
Famous landmarks	luxeadventuretraveler.com/must-see-landmarks/ Search for: "100 must-see landmarks from around the world."
Countries and cities	justfunfacts.com (use the " what are you looking for?" search to search for a specific country) konnecthq.com/geography/ sciencekids.co.nz/sciencefacts/countries.html thefactfile.org (see "Countries")
Travel blogs	swedishnomad.com
World cultures	culturalatlas.sbs.com.au guide.culturecrossing.net (see "get to know your world") theculturetrip.com (a lot about tourist attractions but also cultural things)
New Year's and birthdays	greenglobaltravel.com/celebrate-new-year-traditions-around-the-world/ tasteofhome.com/collection/new-years-eve-traditions-around-world/ coolest-kid-birthday-parties.com/birthday-traditions/ travelstart.co.za/blog/birthday-traditions/

INTERNET RESOURCES

Food around the world	hostelbookers.com/blog/travel/best-breakfast/ tastessence.com/list-of-national-dishes-around-world
People	biography.com biographyonline.net ducksters.com (see "biography") thefamouspeople.com
Records	mostextreme.org guinnessworldrecords.com
Science, space and the universe	kids-fun-science.com ouruniverseforkids.com sciencekids.co.nz (see the "site map") thefactfile.org
Environmental issues	listofenvironmentalissues.com theworldcounts.com

Acknowledgments

I would like to acknowledge and thank those who provided technical support and/or encouragement.

The FedEx team at the Seattle Lake City store provided exceptionally good service for the printing and binding of the many "working versions." Thanks to **Evan's** professionalism and attention to details an error in the book's margins was detected and corrected.

Top Notch Copy & Print produced the cover. It also printed a perfect bound examination copy. It was a pleasure to work with the manager, **Shakeel**.

Stan Levinson, a long-time friend and former EFL/ESL teacher, and **Nilton Hitotuzi**, a former colleague from the Foreign Languages Department at the Federal University of Amazonas, gave valuable suggestions that were incorporated into the book.

I would like to mention two people from Manaus who have had an important influence on my life and thus indirectly on this book: **Professor Ruy Alencar**, founder of the Manaus Brazilian-American Cultural Institute, and **Dona Tereza Assayag,** two of the most remarkable and inspiring people I have had the pleasure of knowing.

My brother, **Jeff**, and my sister, **Maureen**, gave constant and much appreciated encouragement.

My children, **Paula**, **Sergio**, and **David**; my son-in-law, **Thomas**; my daughters-in-law, **Angela** and **Mirella**; and my granddaughters, **Isabella** and **Giovanna,** are an inspiration and gave much support and encouragement.

Finally, my greatest thanks and appreciation go to my wife, **Neusa Maria,** who sadly is not here to share with me the completion of this project.

About the author

Stephen Mark "Gil" Silvers has nearly forty years of classroom experience, having begun his career as a U.S. Information Agency English Teaching Fellow at the Manaus Brazilian-American Cultural Institute (ICBEU) in 1972. There, in addition to teaching, he was responsible (along with two other teachers) for the teacher-training courses.

From 1974 until 2003, he was an instructor in the Federal University of Amazonas's Department of Foreign Languages and Literatures, where he taught all levels of English, as well as American literature and the methodology course for future English teachers.

From 2003 until 2010, he taught English to engineers at a science and technology center for the Manaus Industrial Pole.

He was a presenter at the Twelfth Annual TESOL Convention in Mexico City and made presentations at various BRAZ-TESOL conventions and ENPULI conferences (a Brazilian national conference of university-level English teachers).

He is the author of *Listen and Perform; The Command Book; Point and Touch; Listen and Act* (special editions for the Amazonas state public schools); *Complete English Grammar on CD: The Best Way to TPR any Grammatical Feature in English;* and *Listen and Draw: Easy Drawing Activities for the EFL/ESL Classroom.*

He also has two websites: ESLstation.us (a site for learners) and teachersteve.us (a site for teachers).

He is retired and lives in Seattle where he continues to work on and develop EFL/ESL teaching materials.

www.ingramcontent.com/pod-product-compliance
Lightning Source LLC
Chambersburg PA
CBHW051212290426
44109CB00021B/2422